James Edmund Vincent

The Land Question in South Wales

A defence of the landowners of South Wales and Monmouthshire

James Edmund Vincent

The Land Question in South Wales
A defence of the landowners of South Wales and Monmouthshire

ISBN/EAN: 9783337323882

Printed in Europe, USA, Canada, Australia, Japan

Cover: Foto ©Suzi / pixelio.de

More available books at **www.hansebooks.com**

THE LAND QUESTION IN SOUTH WALES

A DEFENCE OF THE LANDOWNERS OF SOUTH WALES AND MONMOUTHSHIRE

BY

J. E. VINCENT

BARRISTER-AT-LAW

LANDOWNERS' ASSOCIATION OF SOUTH WALES
AND MONMOUTHSHIRE
8 PRINCES STREET, WESTMINSTER
1897

PREFACE.

CURIOUS misunderstandings having arisen concerning the position from which I approached the Welsh Land Question in a former work on behalf of the North Wales Property Defence Association, it appears to be prudent to state that this volume purports to be a brief and necessarily incomplete defence of the Landowners of South Wales and Monmouthshire against an indictment contained in many scattered parts of a Report consisting of 982 Blue-Book pages.

J. E. VINCENT.

8 PRINCES STREET,
   WESTMINSTER.

April 26, 1897.

CONTENTS.

CHAPTER V.

CHAPTER VI.

CHAPTER VII.

APPENDIX.

THE LAND QUESTION IN SOUTH WALES.

CHAPTER I.

By Royal Warrant, given under the hand of Mr. Asquith, the Home Secretary of the day, on the 27th of March 1893, the Royal Commission on Land in Wales and Monmouthshire was appointed " to inquire into the conditions and circumstances under which land in Wales and Monmouthshire is held, occupied, and cultivated, and to report thereon." Of the Commissioners honoured by her Majesty's trust it could not be urged that they were strangers to the country concerned in their inquiry. Lord Carrington, the Chairman, had not, it was true, kept the family estate in Cardiganshire which came to him by inheritance; it had, indeed, been sold almost simultaneously with his succession. But he was, no doubt, familiar with the traditions of that estate ; and, as the Commission grew older, he acquired by purchase from the Earl of Ancaster the mansion and demesne known as Gwydyr Castle, in North Wales, but not any considerable agricultural estate in connection with it. His lordship, however, would probably be the last man to contend, as has been contended on his behalf, that either of these circumstances could justify him in

A

claiming to speak with the authority of experience as a Welsh landowner. Lord Kenyon, descended from the great judge of that name, was and is a considerable landowner on the borders of England and North Wales. Mr. Brynmor Jones, an ex-county court judge and a member of the South Wales Division of the North and South Wales and Chester circuit, a man of pure Welsh descent, could claim close connection with, and much personal experience of, the Principality. Sir John Llewelyn was and is one of the best known landowners in South Wales; Professor Rhys might be described as a very embodiment of the Cymric genius; Mr. Griffiths and Mr. Richard Jones were substantial farmers in Pembrokeshire and Montgomeryshire respectively; Mr. Edwin Grove was known and respected as Chairman of the Monmouthshire County Council and as one familiar with the statistics of great commercial enterprises. The one member of the Commission who had no connection with the Principality was Mr. Seebohm; but his reputation was such that his appointment was a high compliment to the Principality, since in knowledge of the early history of agricultural communities of the United Kingdom he stood, and still stands, absolutely without a rival.

There was, however, be it said with all courteous respect, ground upon which persons opposed, by conviction or from interest, to any revolutionary change in the existing law of landlord and tenant might cavil at the constitution of the Commission. For good or evil the line of political cleavage between the Unionist and the Liberal is tolerably clear and distinct, and common experience teaches us that, given the same set of facts, Tory and Radical will usually differ concerning the course of action which, in their respective opinions, is rendered necessary by those facts. Accordingly it is natural to examine the composition of a Royal Commission with a view to ascertain whether political parties were or were not equally, or nearly equally, represented upon it. Now, of the nine Commissioners in this case Lord Carrington was known as a man of advanced Radical opinions, Mr. Brynmor Jones was the representative of a Gladstonian constituency, Mr. Grove was a Radical Chairman of County Council, Mr. Richard Jones was an active worker in the Radical cause, Mr. Griffiths was a strong Radical, and Professor Rhys a person of uncertain politics. These facts are not mentioned with any idea of casting discredit on the persons named, since honesty of conviction is the common property of both Radical and Tory, but simply because in connection with the Report, and particularly in connection with the recommendations, the political temperaments of its authors are facts which must be taken into consideration ; and these facts, in this particular case, show that the Commission was composed of two parts Radical to one part Unionist.

The Commission thus constituted traversed Wales and Monmouthshire, held ninety-nine public sittings, of which nineteen only were in London, examined 1086 witnesses of various classes, held forty-five private sittings, and agreed upon its Report, so far as it was able to come to any agreement at all, in August of 1896. That Report was published in November of 1896, and it is with it that we have to deal. Our treatment of it, let it be said at once, is treatment measured out from the landowners' point of view, and this short work is the statement issued by the Landowners' Association of South Wales and Monmouthshire of the outlines of their case as proved before the Commission. At the same time, they are fully conscious that nothing is to be gained by overstating a case or by straining facts unduly, and that, although severity of language will be unavoidable on occasion, vehemence of expression is not to be encouraged.

The whole of the Report, however, comprises nearly a thousand pages, of large Blue-book size, and deals with a great variety of subjects of varying qualities and degrees of interest. A large portion of it deals with matters which, except perhaps from the literary, or antiquarian, or historical, or scientific point of view, are in no sense controversial. We are not concerned to inquire into the accuracy or the inaccuracy of the pages relating to those interesting but slightly antique races, the Goidels and the Brythones ; it is a matter of no moment to us how much a Welsh beaver skin cost in the Middle Ages, or whether the ancient nobility of Wales did or did not divert themselves by treating swarms of bees as subjects of the chase. These and kindred topics may be interesting, in varying degrees, to men and women of varying tastes. But the question which lies before us is of a purely practical character. It is our conviction that, when Mr. Gladstone's administration appointed this Commission, it was the intention of Mr. Gladstone's administration that the Commissioners should perform the commonplace, but quite sufficiently onerous task of examining into actual facts with which the Legislature might or might not be able to deal with effect. If this Commission elected to take a wider and more comprehensive view of the terms of reference, and to devote itself to unsystematic research into all kinds of subjects that is no concern of ours. The whole kingdom has to pay the cost, and the miscellany of a thousand pages which is the result is in some measure pleasant in the reading. albeit in many respects inaccurate and incomplete.

Our treatment of the Report is based upon the theory, which we have no doubt to be strictly correct, that this Commission was appointed to inquire into the conditions under which the class of men described as farmers, whether tenants from year to year, or tenants for a fixed period of years, or owners in fee-simple, carry on their industry and trade. We assume that the duty, and the whole duty, of the Commission was meant to consist in discovering, by hearing evidence from the persons interested, whether the conditions of the farmer's life were tolerable or grievous, and whether, if they were grievous, the hardships and difficulties were

such that legislation, framed with due regard to the immut-
able principles of true political science, could alleviate or
remove them. For this assumption there are numerous and
strong grounds. For, first, the task which it would have been
necessary for these men, thus construing the terms of
reference, to perform, was quite large enough to satisfy any
men. To inquire whether, regard being paid to markets and
seasons, the rents paid for farms were reasonable or unreasonable; to ascertain the character of agricultural depres-
sion in Wales and Monmouthshire, to estimate the degrees
of its severity and to investigate its fluctuations; to consider
whether the farming class exercised their energies to the best
advantage and availed themselves of their opportunities to
the full; to see whether they were unjustly treated by landowners or their agents; to find out whether the law of
compensation was adequate or inadequate; to discover
whether favouritism was practised in the choice of tenants;
to examine, in short, into the great question whether landlords
did their duty by their estates and by their tenants—this,
surely, was a duty sufficiently serious to satisfy the ambitions
of any men. Moreover, the preceding history of the Agrarian
agitation, the speeches of Mr. Thomas Ellis, M.P., in the
House of Commons and elsewhere; the Land Bills introduced
by him and by Mr. Bryn Roberts, M.P., respectively; the
Snowdon Speech by Mr. Gladstone, which was the prelude to
the appointment of the Commission, all went plainly to show
that such was the object of its appointment. It was on that
principle that the case for the landowners was shaped before
the Commission from beginning to end. They felt that, so
far as their relation to their agricultural tenants was concerned, they had been placed on their trial, and that it was
their duty to give an account of their stewardship. And
that duty, which involved quite enough of personal exertion
and expense on their parts, they performed steadily, refusing
to be drawn into discussions upon irrelevant topics or to

submit to the arbitrament of the Commission questions with
which it had clearly not been intended that a mixed Commission should deal, and with which, to be plain, this
particular Commission was not competent to deal. Herein
is involved no discourtesy, but a plain statement of manifest
fact ; for it is the simple truth that but one of the Commissioners, and he not a specialist in the law of Real Property,
was competent to enter into those intricate questions of title
concerning which the Commission received a considerable
volume of rather unscientific evidence.

It must be admitted that, from the outset, the Commission
showed a stronger disposition to wander far afield than might
have been expected. But it is now clear that the Commission
itself was well aware that it was going beyond its task.
" Without any doubt," wrote the Commissioners on the first
page of their Report, " we arrived at the conclusion that it was
the conditions and circumstances connected with the ownership and occupation of that land which, for want of a better
term, we call agricultural land, to which we ought, principally, to give our attention." It is suggested that the terms
of reference could not have been construed better or more
intelligently, and that the wandering inquiries of the men
who saw their obvious duty thus plainly and instinctively are
thereby the more difficult to explain. Be that as it may, the
issues are, and were from the beginning, quite plain to Parliament and the public, and, since it is to those issues, and
to the methods pursued in collecting evidence upon them,
that these pages are devoted, quite enough has been said by
way of introduction. ·

Before proceeding to analysis of the Report, or the relevant
portion of it, it is inevitable that a few words, as passionless
as may be possible, should be devoted to the methods pursued
by the Commissioners. Public objection has been made to
criticism of these methods, on the ground that it involves or
implies personal attack upon the characters of individual

Commissioners. But to repeat this objection is to mistake the basis of criticism. It is true, no doubt, that a substantial number of witnesses left the witness-seat with a feeling that they had been harassed and browbeaten in a fashion which was distinctly not fair; it is true also that the strongest supporter of Mr. Brynmor Jones in the vernacular Press, that is to say the *Baner* newspaper, owned by Mr. Thomas Gee, paid him rather an unhappy compliment by describing him as the man who " cut laces out of the skins " of landowners and their witnesses. Where occasion calls for it we shall characterise conduct of this kind without fear and without restraint, since a landowner or an agent is human and has his feelings, just the same as the most august of Royal Commissioners. But it is not desired to lay stress on that aspect of the conduct of the Commissioners, and it will be enough to say for the present that the Commission, which is now *functus officio*, so that each member of it has returned to his ordinary duties and occupations, has left behind it a feeling that several of its members did not hesitate to use their position in an ungenerous and unjust manner, did wound to excess and without reason witnesses with whom they found themselves in disagreement upon matters of opinion, did so far forget themselves upon divers occasions as to fall before the ignoble temptation to play to the gallery.

But, apart from the feeling of just resentment thus produced in the minds of the victims, this really did not very much matter. What is a far more serious affair is the fact, which shall presently be established, that the methods of examination—or non-examination—which were followed were such as to throw very reasonable suspicion upon the materials upon which the Commission was bound to form its judgment. The literature produced by the Commission may be divided into two main parts. There is the evidence, in several bulky volumes; there is the Report. Now, from the scientific point of view, the evidence is by far the more important. Let us imagine a careful and industrious student of politics desirous of approaching this Welsh Land Question with an open mind. To the opinions and recommendations of individual Commissioners as expressed in the Report he would naturally pay no attention until he had made careful inquiry into their intellectual powers, their experience, their character, and their predilections. In this particular case he would come to the conclusion that the judgment of Mr. Seebohm was—we say this with all respect to Sir John Llewelyn and Lord Kenyon and Lord Carrington, and without fear of being misunderstood by them—worth the judgment of all the other Commissioners put together. But he certainly would not accept as final the opinion even of Mr. Seebohm. He would reflect to himself that the Queen does not and cannot send out her trusty and well-beloved Commissioners that they may recommend this or that measure of reform to Parliament, but to discover, and so far as human frailty permits, to state impartially and without favour at the end to Parliament, the precise and complete state of facts. He would feel that even the most unbiased man, acting with that scrupulous impartiality which we have a right to look for in that part of this Report which is made up of summarised evidence, could hardly fail to be led into unconscious error. A little too much shadow here, a little too much light there, emphatic notice of one statement, casual treatment of another, have much influence in determining the general effect of the written statement, and they are errors that are almost unavoidable. Certainly, in the vital part of this Welsh Land Commission's Report, the primary author of the phrases, whosoever he may have been, has not succeeded in avoiding these pitfalls. This, perhaps, is an expression which might be put into a more forcible form if strong criticism were desirable. Let it suffice to say that the draughtsman's efforts to show no bias have not been crowned with complete success.

In these circumstances the political student, or any man of ordinary common sense, can come to no other conclusion than that the evidence, and the evidence alone, is the true mine of information. There only can he expect to find the unvarnished statement of grievance as it came from the mouth of the tenant, the plain statement of defence as it came from the lips of landowner or agent, the clear figures of hereditary succession in tenancy, of reductions of rent, of abatements, of expenditure in improvements and repairs which go to make the positive case for the landowners. That is the real mine of information in which he will, if he be inspired by the genuine zeal after knowledge, be prepared to expend much labour.

Now, it is not suggested for a moment that these nine Royal Commissioners were not entitled, as a matter of law, to disregard the ordinary rules of evidence. They were authorised, no doubt, to collect information in the manner which seemed to them best and most convenient. Let so much be allowed without reserve in their favour. But, on the other hand, it must be said as a matter of duty, without imputing any blame to any individual Commissioner, that the value of the body of evidence collected by them must depend very largely upon the question whether, before that evidence was formally recorded and preserved in the Blue Books, it was subjected to rational tests.

More particularly clear is the necessity of testing evidence in a rational way when the matters in dispute are of such a character as to cause feeling and passion to run high. Such, by universal admission, was the case with which the Welsh Land Commission had to deal. "Differences of race and language, religious and sectarian rivalries, political divisions and social jealousies combined to accentuate, to an extraordinary degree, the feelings engendered by an unequal distribution of wealth and an acute economic crisis . . . Without any intention on our part, and without our being able

to control the matter, the inquiry in some places assumed
the aspect of a warm contention between landlords and tenant
farmers, and indirectly of a contest between the political
parties that struggle for mastery in the State." So the
Commissioners in their Report; nor need we dispute the
statement further than to say that the question whether they
had any control over witnesses was one which depended mainly
upon them. Perhaps if they had possessed the strength of
character and the moral courage which were undoubtedly
required in their position; if they had defined the issues
clearly and had adhered to them; if they had excluded
rigidly all reference to matters which could not be relevant
to any conceivable issue; if they had firmly resisted evidence
relating solely to questions of personal conduct and character;
then, probably, they would have had no difficulty in control-
ling the course of the inquiry. This mild complaint, this
melancholy expression of sorrow that the inquiry followed
lines which the Commissioners could by no means control, is
in truth a very simple and childlike confession of weakness.
So striking is it, indeed, that we venture to retort upon the
Commission by inverting an observation made in public by
Mr. Commissioner Brynmor Jones and turning it upon the
Commission. Mr. Brynmor Jones was good enough to
explain to the *Times* newspaper that if counsel for landowners
could not cross-examine effectually, the fault did not lie with
the Commissioners. That observation was in revolt against the
despotism of facts, for the simple reason that the Commission,
exercising a discretion which is not questioned, declined to
permit counsel, or anybody else than a Commissioner, to cross-
examine at all by word of mouth; permitting merely written
questions to be administered; and to call such questions
" cross-examination " is simply to misuse language. On the
other hand, the Commission had undoubted authority to
control and direct the course of its own inquiry; and if it
failed to exercise that authority while, by its own profession,

it was desirous of so doing, the fault lay not in want of authority but in lack of capacity on the part of the Commission. The real doubt is whether the political cast given to the inquiry was in truth contrary to the wishes of the Commissioners. To be candid, we do not think it was distasteful to them, and, upon a survey of the evidence, we venture to say that individual Commissioners, notably Mr. Brynmor Jones, Mr. Richard Jones, and, in the matter of anti-clerical prejudice, Mr. Griffiths, rivalled any of the persons who marshalled evidence before them in importing political passions into the inquiry.

This was, perhaps, a pity, though an open fight of this kind may sometimes work benefit by supplying a vent for the turgid gas of political feeling; but it certainly does not lie in the mouths of the majority of the Commissioners to complain that, in spite of them, the inquiry assumed a political colour, when in fact they helped to give to it that colour. Moreover, upon this point they have fallen into a serious error of fact, and they must be set right. Speaking of the eagerness with which the inquiry was followed by the Welsh people in terms which are, in our judgment, exaggerated, they write (Report, p. 2): "No doubt this was to some extent caused by the political aspect given to our inquiry, and by *the intervention everywhere of a political organisation on the part of the landlords*, and at most places on the part of the tenants." Whether this be true of the gentlemen who marshalled the case for the malcontent tenants, it is not for us to say, but we are constrained to observe that the words which we have italicised are absolutely without foundation in fact in the ordinary sense of words, without a colour of foundation, and contrary to evidence given before the Commission, so far as the South Wales and Monmouthshire Association is concerned. That association was the only association of landowners represented before the Commission in South Wales.

In North Wales there was colour, but no real foundation, for the suggestion. In other words, although the members of the North Wales Property Defence Association include persons of every shade of political opinion except that which favours Land Leagues, the secretary of that association, the late Mr. George Owen, was in another capacity a political organiser on the Conservative side. Still, the North Wales Property Defence Association has no connection with any political organisation, and has often declined to take any part in movements having a political complexion. In the case of the Landowners' Association of South Wales and Monmouthshire, the suggestion or charge, if charge it be, of political basis of organisation is a sheer invention. Let us be quite plain. In a classical sense every association of men, even a cricket club, is political, since man is, as our old friend Aristotle discovered some hundreds of years ago, πολιτικὸν ζῶον, a living creature calculated to be one of a community. But this was not the meaning in which the Commissioners used the word "political"; they intended to convey the impression that the association referred to was connected with party politics. That impression is absolutely false. The Association had its origin in the appointment of the Welsh Land Commission; its object is the perfectly legitimate one of defending the rights of property; it is expressly non-political; its members represent all shades of opinion in the political world; it does not attempt to exercise any influence over elections; its secretary, who represented it before the Commission at every public sitting, has never been a member of any political organisation more serious in character than the Chatham Club, which was youthful and pleasantly convivial. He left that club at the mature age of twenty-two, and it is only on rare occasions that he can be persuaded to vote even at a Parliamentary election. Thus neglecting his duties as a citizen, he is the least political man imaginable.

The preceding words are not a digression, and therefore need no excuse after the manner of Lawrence Sterne. Their purpose is to lead to the contention that the conditions under which the Welsh Land Commission worked were such that they ought to have been more than commonly careful to subject evidence to rational tests. They were unable, they protest, to prevent their inquiry from taking a political cast; they encouraged, we contend, the political spirit by showing it themselves; they thought, quite erroneously, but it must be assumed, honestly, that landowners and tenants were represented before them by political organisations; they frequently asked witnesses what their politics were; they saw the passions of men exhibited before them with increasing force every day. Now, the game of politics has never been a very clean or scrupulous game. The terms " stupid Tory," and " beastly Radical," the old story that a Cardiganshire man, having all but exhausted his vocabulary of abuse upon a perverse donkey, roused him to a gallop by calling him " Tori bach," sufficiently indicate the tone of political controversy at its worst. It is matter of common knowledge that every General Election is so prolific of gross and baseless personal libels that members of Parliament have been compelled to protect themselves against one another by special enactment. In fact, if the devil is the father of lies politics are the forcing-houses of them.

The inquiry, then, took a political cast. It was natural to expect a large crop of falsehoods; and no man who followed the course of the evidence given before the Commission will deny that, mixed up with a great mass of valuable facts, a huge volume of sheer falsehoods came before the Commission. We need not specify instances. The thousands of pages of evidence contain numerous examples of serious accusations which were not merely denied, but absolutely disproved by evidence which could not be doubted, sometimes even by documentary evidence signed by the accuser's own hand;

the Blue Books are marred in countless cases by charges not
only irrelevant to any conceivable issue, but impossible on
the face of them.

In a word, the evidence, which ought to be the most
valuable fruit of the work of the Welsh Land Commission,
which ought to be a rich treasury of golden information,
cannot be regarded as established and trustworthy. Brought
face to face with it, the political inquirer, the member of
Parliament desirous of finding out the truth concerning this
Welsh Land Question (which some declare to be of deadly
interest, while others hold it to be mere make-believe) is like
an assayer of gold who is confronted with a mass of mixed ore,
and rigidly prohibited from applying to it any scientific test
by which to distinguish the base metal from the true.

Complaints to this effect were made often, and with just
indignation, during the long life of the Commission, and they
were met by the short-sighted answer that the Commission
was not legally bound by the accepted law of evidence. No
sane man ever said that it was so bound; no reasonable
person would contend that a rigid application of the strict
law of evidence was, in the case of non-controversial matters,
necessary or even desirable. For example, it would have been
absurd to insist on evidence at first hand, although, as a
matter of fact, it was available and formally offered if
demanded, in the case of the statistical returns concerning
the rise and fall of rents and like matters furnished by the
secretaries of the Landowners' Associations in North and
South Wales and in Monmouthshire; and equally absurd
would it have been to press for strict proof of much of the
evidence given on the other side.

But it is very plain, on the face of the evidence recorded,
that many of the statements made and the whole of the
charges of personal misconduct or dishonesty levelled
against individuals were of such a character that, unless they
were able to pass through strict tests, they could carry no

weight. Those strict tests happen to be embodied in the law of evidence, most of which is not the creation of any statute, but the accumulated result of the experience of man in civilised communities. Man has learned that certain rules must be applied before it can be ascertained whether a witness is accurate or inaccurate (which is a matter of intellectual capacity rather than of morality), or whether he is telling the truth or a deliberate falsehood. Experience shows beyond question that many witnesses make mistakes; that many, a less number, lie with elaborate precision; and that an inquiry conducted under circumstances of passion, such as surrounded this particular inquiry, and when falsehoods can be told freely and without fear of punishment (for the law of slander has narrow limits and the law of perjury had no application) is manifestly liable to be prolific of untruth. The Commission declined to apply those well-known tests. It is true that they were not legally bound to apply them. But every consideration of reason and fair-play was obligatory upon them. They neglected those considerations. But in making this statement we are actuated by no desire to speak evil of the Commissioners. Their capacity, their honesty of purpose, their character, are matters of small moment to the world at large; but the fact that this mountain of so-called evidence, this accumulation of alleged evidence, which is all that public opinion can go by, has never been properly tested, and cannot be properly tested now or ever, is serious, lamentable, and irretrievable.

No apology is called for in connection with the particularity with which this subject is being treated, for the importance of it is of the most essential quality, and the question of the validity and truthfulness of the evidence goes to the root of the whole matter. Here, in 982 pages, is the great literary edifice of the Report. Below it, in the shape of foundation, is the evidence spread over five or six times as many pages. Our submission is that the edifice is liable to collapse at any

moment; that the foundations upon which it stands may be
wide, but that they are not deep; that they rest not on the
solid rock of truth and certainty, but upon the shifting
quicksands of uncertainty. To prove this is to invalidate the
whole Report and to demonstrate to the impartial mind that,
save as a mere expression of personal opinion, the recommendations of the majority are not worthy to carry any
weight. It will be necessary, before this volume is ended, to
call attention to particular cases of unfair treatment of
witnesses by the majority of the Commissioners; to show that,
on the face of their Report, they have reached conclusions
upon matters of fact (upon the qualifications of land-agents,
for example) not warranted by, and not in harmony with, that
which they are pleased to call evidence. But it is more
important by far to be able to show that the whole of the
evidence as it stands has not passed those tests, and can now
never be subjected to those tests, which alone could give it a
title to be believed. We cannot tell whether we are dealing
with dreams, with mere fictions, the fruit of malicious imagination, or with facts; and facts are the only things that
matter.

Lest room should be left for doubt, it is prudent to append
to the general statement the particular details of complaint.
It shall be done at once. When a man went into the witness-
box, or to the table, and, as was the common practice before
this Commission, read a statement of grievance and complaint,
the first thing which sensible persons wanted to know was
whether he was telling his own story or one which somebody
else had put on paper for him. That instinctive desire was
shown by one of the Commissioners during the first week of
the sittings of the Commission in South Wales. It certainly
never entered into the mind of counsel for landowners, who
had put this witness in the box, that he could venture to
question this absolutely proper line of cross-examination. On
the contrary, condemned as he was to grope in the dark after

the rules of practice which the Commission was likely to follow, he determined to use these questions as a model and an example. When next an exuberant witness appeared on the other side, full of poetical phrases and florid epithets, it seemed good to place these questions, copied from the model provided by the Commissioners, before him also for answer. Divers Commissioners, however, resented the questions (they had forgotten their original source) as an outrage upon and an insult to a poor tenant farmer. Counsel, like Brer Rabbit, lay low. The questions were then disallowed, in a haughty tone, as improper. Counsel then proceeded to point out to the chairman in writing the true origin of these questions, and, after the luncheon adjournment, he learned, to his intense surprise, that by way of getting out of a difficulty which, so far, affected the evidence of one witness only, the Commissioners had agreed upon a rule which could not fail to invalidate more or less the evidence of every individual among the thousand witnesses to be called thereafter. For the Commission resolved, and counsel took good care that they should not break through their own rule later, that under no circumstances should any person, whether a member of the public or a Commissioner, make inquiry of any witness as to the manner in which his evidence had been prepared. Every man accustomed to sift evidence, every lawyer, every magistrate, every man who has occasion, in any walk of life, to distinguish between truth and falsehood, will say without hesitation that, *by the passing of this almost incredible rule, the first and most elementary test of evidence was abolished and destroyed.* From that day forward the personal honour and character of a witness were the only guarantees that his evidence was not simply invented by the political agent, the lawyer, or the organiser, who brought him forward. So incredible is this rule, that it seems necessary to add that, on many occasions, individual Commissioners tried to break through it, and were checked by written protests by counsel for landowners, who had cards ready bearing the necessary words of remonstrance.

The excuse for the rule was that inquiry into the sources of evidence would have taken time ; but, in truth, the knowledge that such inquiry could not be made unquestionably contributed incalculably to the volume of evidence offered ; and it may be added that an ounce of evidence which has stood the proper tests is worth more than a ton of so-called evidence that virtually has not been tested at all.

This is the principal weakness which underlies the whole of the books of evidence. But there were others. The Commissioners cannot be acquitted of having admitted great quantities of hearsay statements, where direct evidence might easily have been obtained, upon serious questions of character and conduct. Not all hearsay was objectionable of course. There was no strong reason why a particular individual should not be received, as many were received, as the spokesman of a district or of a meeting, to give expression to their feeling upon general questions, such as the desirability of a Land Court, or the necessity of amending the Agricultural Holdings Act. It would have been more businesslike, no doubt, if such spokesmen had produced copies of resolutions passed at the meetings in question ; but let that pass ; it is not worthy of serious mention by the side of the other kinds of hearsay that were admitted. Over and over again, both in South Wales and in North, men were permitted in so many words to tell other persons' stories for them ; to say that So-and-so was evicted for political reasons, that another did not receive a penny of compensation when he left his farm, although he had spent hundreds upon it, and so forth *ad infinitum*. Now, this kind of evidence is open to every kind of suspicion. It may be untrue from the beginning, and the alleged victim may have misled the willing witness ; on the other hand, the willing witness may have mistaken or deliberately misrepresented the alleged victim. Besides, the man who goes into

the box to tell another man's story cannot be cross-examined
effectually, however honest he may be, simply because he
knows nothing more than he has been told and cannot answer
yes or no to questions of which the answers may explain the
whole matter and dispose of the alleged grievance.

No parallel for this practice can be found in practical life
outside the history of the Welsh Land Commission. Newspapers are, for the most part, made up of course of hearsay
statements; but the reporter who repeats the hearsay is
checked by the knowledge that a series of mistakes will
involve him in the loss of his livelihood, whereas the man
who created a sensation before the Welsh Land Commission
was accounted a high-minded patriot. Moreover, a newspaper
is obnoxious to libel actions, whilst a witness before the
Commission might give free rein to his imagination so long
as he refrained from imputing to a man an indictable offence,
or from saying that which brought pecuniary damage to a
man, or from slandering him in his trade or business. The
really analogous case would be seen if counsel were permitted
to give evidence for their absent clients; if, for example, Mr.
Marshall Hall had been permitted, at a recent trial at the
Old Bailey, to give his version of what the deceased boy Kast
would have said. To imagine that any court of law would
allow or any jury would listen to evidence of that character
is to imagine the impossible. There is not, indeed, a practising lawyer who has not known many times, and to his
cost, how vast is the difference between the sunny statement
of his witness, as it appeared in his brief, and the chequered
aspect of the evidence of that witness when he steps out of
the box after cross-examination.

The remaining weaknesses of the practice of the Commission may be summed up in a paragraph. They frequently
admitted at the outset verbal statements as to the effect and
contents of written documents which were not produced.
They admitted hand-made and undated copies of alleged

agreements (names of parties omitted), of which it was said
that they were contracts out of the Act of 1883.   One such
was found subsequently to be dated 1875! But on this
point they were inconsistent, for, when a clergyman at Rhyl
tendered a copy of a lease, he was sternly told that copies
would not be admitted.   They allowed a malcontent witness
to hand up to them privately the names of six alleged victims
of Lord Windsor (that is to say, they gave him leave to do so,
but nobody knows whether he did it or not) ; they informed
a sub-agent of Miss Talbot, who desired to submit privately
the name of his informant, that under no circumstances could
they accept confidential communications.

That is the kind of Commission with which Welsh landowners had to deal ; that is the way in which the material
upon which this colossal Report professes to be founded was
collected and raked together.   It cannot be contended that it
was not a duty to set forth these plain facts before looking at
what these Commissioners have to say and what they presume
to recommend.

CHAPTER II

LET us now proceed to deal with those portions of the Report which have a practical as distinguished from a merely literary and antiquarian interest.

First it is to be noted that, while there is a Majority Report and a Minority Report, it is difficult, if not impossible, to ascertain with how much of the observations of the majority the minority agree. The minority, composed of Lord Kenyon, Sir John Llewelyn and Mr. Seebohm, leave us in considerable doubt upon this point, which is unfortunate; and to show how unfortunate it is, we quote from the opening of the Minority Report.

"We have been anxious, as far as we honestly could, to agree with our colleagues in the report of the facts which have come before the Commission and in the general inferences to be drawn from them. And with that view we have signed the first part of the Report as a painstaking endeavour to place on record a broad view of the conditions under which land is held and cultivated in Wales. *There may be parts of the Report as to which, in our view, undue regard may have been paid to statements of those naturally under political bias, and undue prominence given to matters more or less the subject of political agitation. We have regretted the frequent introduction of personal matters by reference to individual cases by name. However carefully a short statement of facts, often imperfectly disclosed in the evidence, may be drawn, it is impossible to avoid the danger of not fully representing aspects of the case which to the individual may be of personal importance as more or less implying moral blame; and we should deeply regret if in the statement of these cases in the Report any unjust moral aspersion should have been unintentionally cast upon any individual, whether landlord or tenant. With these reservations as regards this part of the Report, we have not thought it needful to withhold our general concurrence."*

Now, the first point that strikes the mind on perusal of this introductory paragraph is that no man can say, and the minority of the Commissioners themselves find it difficult to distinguish, how many of the statements in the Report, apart from the recommendations, are to be taken as unanimous. If the authors of the Report, or the partial endorsers of it, are in this difficulty, it must be abundantly clear that any individual not a member of the Commission who attempts to mark out the boundary line between unanimity and difference in this wilderness of words must fail ignominiously. That is, as has been observed, a grave misfortune, especially from the point of view of those who hold that the views of Mr. Seebohm, Lord Kenyon and Sir John Llewelyn carry considerable weight.

Next, the reader cannot fail to remember that when this important paragraph was written the "painstaking endeavour" to summarise the evidence fairly was before the eyes of those who deemed it necessary to preface their own observations with these words of warning prudence. What, then, do we gather? That the main body of the vital part of the Report came into being from the pen or the mouth of some person or persons, and that, whether there was one author or more than one, neither Sir John Llewelyn, Lord Kenyon, or Mr. Seebohm had any share in the authorship. No one of these gentlemen, assuredly, is capable of describing work wholly or partly his own as a "painstaking endeavour."

For the rest, the paragraph plainly indicates that, in the opinion of these honourable and responsible men, the readers of the Report must be on their guard against undue regard paid to the statements of those naturally under political bias, undue prominence given to matters more or less the subject of political agitation, unnecessary introduction of personalities, inadequate and inaccurate summaries of evidence. Far be it from us to dispute this opinion reached by men of notorious impartiality and so conciliatory in disposition that they did not withhold "general concurrence" from what had been written by others. On the contrary, it is a part of the present task to justify the warning given by the minority to show that a distinctly partisan bias runs through the whole of the vital portion of the Report and through part of the Introduction; to point out that sentence after sentence, without embodying any direct statement of fact that can be disproved, has a sting in the tail of it; and to show that the summaries of evidence, upon which Mr. Thomas Ellis, M.P., appeared, in his recent Carmarthen speech, to set great store, are in many respects, and most particularly in reference to the qualifications of agents, more than accidentally imperfect. For the present, however, it is enough to observe that, for dignified and uncompromising condemnation of the method pursued in drafting the only part of the Report which has reference to the circumstances of the present day or possesses any practical interest, the well-considered words of Mr. Seebohm, Sir John Llewelyn, and Lord Kenyon leave absolutely nothing to be desired.

And now let us make a "painstaking endeavour" to summarise, as briefly and accurately as may be within our capacity, those parts of the Report which, whether unanimous or not, are of real interest, and to specify the recommendations of the entire body, of the majority, and of the minority; dealing with these matters as they come and in the order of convenience.

Upon certain points in the Report of which there is strong
reason to complain it is to be feared that unanimity must be
predicated.   And this, we take it, must be said of the Introduction, which contains sundry passages highly objectionable
to all friends of the present system of landownership to which
it is not possible for them to assent.

The most objectionable of these is contained in the ninth
paragraph (page 9), in respect of the allegation that tenants
were afraid to come forward and give evidence. " But in
our judgment we feel bound to say that not simply a small
number of exceptionally timid and prudent men, but a very
large proportion of the tenant-farmers in each district were
deterred from coming forward to give evidence by fear of
incurring the displeasure of the landlord, and therefore
possibly of receiving notice to quit, or, at any rate, being
placed in a disadvantageous position as regards him and his
agent."   They then are kind enough to say that they are
sure no considerable number of landowners would be
prejudiced against a tenant because he gave " candid and
accurate evidence."   Then they exhort landowners not to do
anything which can possibly lead to a suspicion, no matter
how groundless, of this kind.

The inference is obvious.   The landowner who desires to
secure from the Commissioners a character for prudence must
never, whatsoever may happen in the future, whatsoever
provocation may be offered to him, take in his own interests
any step which may be disadvantageous to the public-spirited
tenants who came before the Commission.   It follows from
this doctrine that to have given evidence, true or false, is, if the
view of the Commissioners is to be upheld, to have acquired a
property near akin in nature to perpetuity of tenure.   " We
are sure," say the Commissioners in effect, " that landlords
will not punish ; but they must avoid the very suspicion
of punishment"; and this means that tenants are to be
cosseted and favoured for no other reason than that, having

an opportunity offered to them, they have chosen to make, out of mere animosity and malignance, and without regard to the relevance of their observations, serious attacks upon the characters of the owners or managers of the land which they occupy or have occupied.

It would be interesting to learn whether the accusations, quite irrelevant to the real issues which the Commission had to try, made by a Mr. Evans against Lord Windsor's agent, Mr. Forrest, ought in the opinion of our tender-hearted Commissioners to entitle the said Mr. Evans to perpetuity of tenure. It would be instructive also to learn whether there are any limits to the theory that the practice of back-biting a landlord, aptly described by Lord Morris in the House of Lords by the phrase " domestic treachery," entitles a man not only to the negative advantage of freedom from punishment, but also to the positive benefit of substantial reward.

The next reference in the sermon (for the whole of the phraseology savours of "the word of exhortation") is to certain evictions for political reasons alleged to have taken place after the elections of 1859 and 1868. With these allegations it is not proposed to deal in detail, for two excellent reasons. In the first place they are allegations in relation to which the Commissioners, if they considered the topic material, had an absolute right, not merely in law, but also in reason, to accept hearsay evidence. But it followed from this fact that the allegations were in themselves liable to that doubt which must always attach to hearsay, and that they were far more easy to make than to meet. One cannot prove that a man now dead did not tell Thomas Jones that a landlord, now dead, did not give him notice to quit because he refused to give a vote contrary to his political convictions. That, at any rate is plain ; for one cannot call the dead landlord back to life for examination upon his original motives. Nor is it possible in 1897 to discover whether, forty or fifty years ago, there was, either in the mind of the landlord or in the condition of the evicted tenant's holding, something other than politics which might explain the eviction. Nor, unhappily, can it be denied that, in days which were less enlightened than ours, there were evictions which proceeded from political motives. Those were times in which tenancy was regarded as a privilege. They were times in which men held the opinion—and the present writer for one is not going to say that it was an unreasonable opinion—that they were entitled to surround themselves with their supporters and friends. But we are entitled to say that this principle, even if it be regarded as obsolete in these days, prevailed and was acted upon in England as well as in Wales. We have a clear right to say also that the evidence given on the subject was inevitably open to suspicion on the ground of vagueness and because it could not be tested; and that much of it showed signs of a natural tendency to exaggeration. But the true answer is that these evictions of ancient days, of which the Commission makes a prodigal use, were quite irrelevant to the present problem, if indeed problem there be. If there was tyranny of that kind thirty and forty years ago, such tyranny is impossible now. The Ballot Act has been passed in the interval. By the universal admission of all parties, it is absolutely effectual. It is impossible to discover whether a man has voted for the blue or for the yellow, and therefore impossible to punish him for his vote. Frankly, it is impossible to believe that any reasoning being in 1897 can stand in terror of a recurrence of the events of those bygone years; if there be such men then their timidity is incurable and constitutional. They have absolute protection, and that must suffice for them. But it is a piece of legitimate criticism to add that the Commissioners who have to hark so far back for their arguments must have been sorely distressed to find any arguments at all.

In connection with the same subject, that of groundless and

unreasoning fear, the Commissioners, in a portion of their
Report which bears the appearance of unanimity, deal with a
point of vital importance to the landowners and the estate
agents of South Wales and Monmouthshire. No apology is
made for dealing with this subject in some detail, since it is a
plain duty to defend a body of men who are held in just
esteem and regard against an accusation which is of an
obviously grave nature. It is the kind of accusation which
ought by no means to be made unless the grounds of it have
been tested with anxious care ; and certainly it is such a charge
that to make it, after the evidence supporting it has been
submitted to an impartial authority and has been authorita-
tively declared to be inadequate, is nothing short of scandalous.
It will be remembered that, during the course of the inquiry,
certain witnesses, hailing from South Wales for the most
part, came forward to allege that they had been punished,
damnified, or otherwise injured by reason of evidence given
by them to the disadvantage of the owners of the land which
they happened to hold under agreement. The allegations,
apart from the flimsy evidence by which they were supported,
were of grave importance for, if they had been justified, they
would have provided some ground for saying that the vague
fear to give evidence, to which sundry witnesses testified,
was not in truth unreasoning. And they were the more
important in that they were a boon to the local newspapers,
which found readers where the official reports of evidence
found none, and were circulated far and wide.

What, then, was the course taken by the Commissioners in
relation to an important question affecting the characters and
the honour of a large body of gentlemen who had the common
right to be regarded as innocent until they had been proved
to be guilty ? It was, in a word, extraordinary. The Commissioners, as is incontestably demonstrated by the Report,
positively assumed the likelihood of guilt in landowners before
they took the first step in their general inquiry and, when

allegations had been made and had been laughed to scorn by
unprejudiced officials, the Commissioners adhered to an attitude of suspicion which had been ignoble from the beginning.
Not only did they presume the guilt of landowners before a
syllable had been said against them, but also they persisted
in asserting their guilt after they had been proved to be
innocent. It was surely by inadvertence that Lord Kenyon,
Sir John Llewelyn, and Mr. Seebohm assented to proceedings
and appended their signatures to a Report which can bear no
other interpretation than this.

The statement which has just been made must be verified
without delay, for in itself it is serious and deliberate, and
the justification of it will go a long way to indicate the temper
and the prejudices of the Commissioners with whom Welsh
landowners had to deal.

"We could not help contemplating the possibility of
attempts being made to intimidate witnesses from coming
before us, or to injure them for doing so, though we believed
that this was not likely to happen" (Report, page 12). To
be plain, we cannot appreciate the difficulty of resisting the
contemplation of this possibility. It appears to us to have its
origin in groundless and cynical suspicion. It seems to us
that we are justified in saying that at the bar of a Commission
which entertained this suspicion before a single witness had
been heard, the class of persons upon whom that suspicion
was thrown could not hope for that fair trial which, in fact,
they did not obtain. The sentence quoted was made public
in the Report for the first time ; but the feeling in which it
was penned animated the Commission from the beginning.
The Chairman, as the Report points out in a boasting mood,
adopted a novel and curious method of encouraging witnesses
at each new place of sitting. It was his custom to recite an
imposing proclamation describing, in the first place, the pains
and penalties which might be suffered by witnesses who had
the temerity to come forward and give evidence. The stereo-

typed proclamation ended with the words " We desire therefore (and it is our duty to do so) to point out that the
Witnesses Protection Act of 1892 affords a remedy adequate
to meet any ordinary case."

In passing we may observe a curious omission. The
Chairman, in this curious way, urged witnesses to come forward, but he omitted, out of tender regard for their feelings,
to impress upon them the necessity of testifying to the truth.
He was accurate in saying that the Act in question afforded
an adequate remedy in ordinary cases, but he omitted to
warn witnesses that an ordinary case is assumed to be that of
a truthful witness, and that the statute affords no protection
to false testimony given in bad faith. But it appears from the
Report that the Commissioners, or some of them, were not
satisfied with the sincerity of the proclamation which they
authorised to be made with so much precious solemnity. They
go on to say, " We were [presumably at the beginning of the
inquiry], and are, well aware that the language of the statute
is such, and the difficulty of proving an offence under it to
the satisfaction of a court of law is so great, that many
possible cases of wrongful treatment of persons for having
given evidence before a Royal Commission must escape
punishment."

The situation in which the Commissioners thus place themselves is grimly entertaining. Firstly, out of the fertility of
their collective imagination, they evolve dangers; secondly,
they warn witnesses of the existence of these imaginary
dangers; thirdly, they tell witnesses to be of good courage
because the Act provides an adequate remedy; fourthly, they
confess that they knew all the while that the Act was of no
value. If this were a case in which personages less august
were involved the plain man would be disposed to say that
persons who said that a statute afforded sufficient protection
when they felt perfectly certain that it did nothing of the
kind could hardly claim that they had dealt with their

audiences in good faith. The case is similar to that of a countryman saying to a stranger in winter "the ice may bear, or may give way, but it does not matter much, for there are no more than two feet of water in any part of the pond," when, in fact, the countryman well knew the depth to be ten feet or more in places.

As for the criticism of the Act, it is childish in the last degree. Its defect, which is never likely to be remedied outside a lunatic asylum, is that the prosecution must prove a case against the prisoner before conviction can be obtained. Nobody, except the queen in "Alice in Wonderland," ever dreamed of basing a criminal enactment on any other principle, and no despotic monarch has ever attempted to follow the method of "sentence first and trial afterwards" without forcing his subjects into rebellion. It is true that the prosecution has in this, as in many other classes of crime, to prove the motive of the accused. But there is nothing mysterious in that, since it is a well-known rule of law that a man must be held to intend the consequences of his own actions, and, in the absence of adequate explanation, to have been animated by the motive which his subsequent actions suggest. In a case under this Act the Crown would have to prove, in the first place, that the evidence had been given and the witness had suffered at the hands of the accused. There would then be several conceivable defences. First, the accused might prove that the evidence given was deliberately untrue; that would have been the defence in several cases alleged before the Commission. Secondly, he might show that the punishment was never inflicted. Either of these defences, if established, would ensure acquittal. Thirdly, the accused might not merely say that his motive in inflicting the punishment had no reference to the evidence given, but also corroborate his statement by placing in evidence substantial facts in confirmation of it. This last would naturally be the most difficult defence to establish.

The Commissioners are, however, not satisfied with puerile criticism of the statute which they solemnly declared to be effectual for protection : they distinctly declare that it has not been effectual, and that punishment has been inflicted ; they say in effect that Welsh gentlemen, or some of them, have been guilty of crime in connection with the proceedings before the Commission. That the Commissioners publish this scandalous libel in a sentence in which they confess that they have no right to express an opinion at all, is only character- istic of their methods. " We have had to decide, therefore, how far it is right for us to express an opinion as to the criminality of the persons complained of, and *have come to the conclusion that it does not lie within our province, deeply as we regret that in any case the law should have failed to give the protection intended by the Act.*" The italics are ours, and they are used to emphasise the inconsistency of men who, in one breath, condemn, as criminal, actions upon which they confess that they have no right to express an opinion. It may be added that the distinction between the law and the Act is meaningless. For the purpose of protection of witnesses the Act is the law, and the law is the Act, and Parliament intended that the Act should punish those who were proved to be guilty, and none others.

But the point is that the Commissioners solemnly aver, although in some cases they curtailed and refused to hear the case for the defence after hearing the prosecution in full, that intimidation and punishment of witnesses were practised. They express the same opinion, in a sentence purporting to contain their impressions as to the meaning of the Act, the said sentence being so crammed with innuendoes that it cannot be called high-minded, and at the same time so art- lessly expressed that it is possible to trace the particular case which the framer of the sentence had in mind. " But we were distinctly under the impression that, in the true con- struction of the Act, any action by a landlord adverse to a

tenant who had given evidence before us for which any
capricious, trivial, and wholly inadequate reasons were given,
would certainly *primâ facie* come within its terms and at any
rate throw on a landlord the onus of justifying his action."
The " distinct impression " is merely a ponderous explanation
of the obvious meaning of the statute ; the distinct intention,
which is quite another matter, is to assert in a manner not
magnanimous, because it is indefinite, that a tenant has been
punished by a landlord for giving evidence, that the landlord
has given trivial and inadequate reasons for his conduct, that
the Solicitor to the Treasury has declined to institute a prosecution, and that an appeal to the Home Secretary has
produced no result in the shape of a prosecution.

A little patience and careful application of the method of
exhaustion, combined with a knowledge of the indiscreet
utterances of the Commissioners on various occasions, render
it possible to point to the particular case which the Commissioners had in mind in framing these observations, and
justify the statement that the same Commissioners who
declare that to decide whether conduct is criminal or not have,
in fact, expressed a decided view that two honourable gentlemen conspired together to punish, and in fact did punish, a
witness for giving evidence.

Observe, they allege action adverse to a tenant for giving
evidence by his landlord, who gave explanatory evidence by
way of defence. This excludes the ridiculous but irritating
accusation made by Ben Maddy, the rabbit-catcher, against
Mr. Thurston Bassett, a master of hounds. Mr. Bassett, it is
true, is a landlord, and made as much explanation as the
Commission, which had heard the accusation in full, was disposed to permit. In this case, be it observed, Maddy's complaint was based on the alleged statements of divers persons,
whom the Commission refused to hear in full, although they
had been taken all the way from Glamorganshire to Brecon
at Mr. Bassett's expense, whereas Maddy was conveyed at the

expense of the country. But Maddy was not Mr. Bassett's tenant; so that cock will not fight. Nor can the reference be to the ingenuous tenant of Mr. Charles Matthias, who, after testifying that Mr. Matthias paid his rates for him, alleged that, after and in consequence of the testimony, Mr. Matthias ceased to show that particular form of generosity. For in this case the landlord treated the Commission with contempt by not attempting any explanation at all. Probably his feeling in the matter—assuming the story to be true—was that even the newest Act of Parliament could not be so construed as to compel a landlord or anybody else to encourage domestic treachery by gratuitous reward. Nor can the reference be to the ardent Board School master of somewhere near Lampeter in " the sweet shire of Cardigan," for his complaint was made against a School Board and a bank. The School Board, he alleged, turned him out of his office and took him back again; the bank made him pay his overdraft, and addressed to him a letter with the common form of which many men have the misfortune to be familiar. But in this case the relation of landlord and tenant does not appear to have been disturbed, since it did not exist.

Internal evidence shows that the reference is clearly to. what the chairman of the day was pleased to describe as " the very distressing case of Mr. John Thomas," and in relation to . which the chairman ended his little oration of sympathy by an expression of the opinion of the Commission that no . adequate explanation or reason had been given for the treatment measured out to Mr. John Thomas aforesaid.

An entirely factitious importance has been given to this case in Parliament and in the Press, partly perhaps because Mr. John Thomas, the alleged victim, was the brother of Mr. D. Lleufer Thomas, the secretary of the Commission. So far has the agitation concerning "the very distressing case of Mr. John Thomas " proceeded that an endeavour has been made to establish him in the position of a martyr, new style ;

C

that is to say, the kind of martyr for whom a public
subscription is started. Whether this enterprise was suc-
cessful or not the present writer is unable to state; but
he has his doubts, since he remembers a shrewd saying of
the late Dr. Herber Evans, an eminent Nonconformist
divine and orator, to the effect that the way to the Welsh-
man's heart is short, but the way to his pocket is long.
Possibly, however, the appeal may have reached the ears and
the pockets of generous Englishmen.

Be that as it may, the case is of sufficient importance to
demand attention and investigation; and the facts, so far as
they are common ground, are these. Mr. John Thomas was
tenant of a farm called Troed-yr-Rhiw, about twelve miles
from Carmarthen, under Mr. Gerwyn Jones, an owner of
considerable property in the district. He gave evidence on
the 21st of April 1894, in Welsh. The complaints made in
the evidence, of which the English version is of considerable
literary merit, were, on the whole, normal and so phrased as
to cover a whole parish. The personal grievances of Mr.
Thomas appeared to consist in a belief that the agent, a
Welsh-speaking banker, was "not a suitable or competent
intermediary between the landlord and his tenants"; in a
statement that, at the bidding of Mr. Gerwyn Jones's father,
he had deserted the sect of Independents and had become an
attendant at Church, and that he had been injured by the
resumption on the part of the landlord of nine acres of his
holding (for which the landlord paid £14 per annum) for the
purposes of a rabbit warren and so forth. On the 25th, Mr.
Watkins, the agent, replied at Lampeter. So far the matter
seemed to be free from any extraordinary features.

But at a subsequent meeting of the Commission, Mr. John
Thomas came forward to state that he had received notice to
quit, and that he believed this notice to have been given to
him solely because he had given evidence. The accusation
of crime thus made against Mr. Gerwyn Jones and Mr.

Watkins was the more serious in that the accuser, albeit himself in no degree superior to the small farmers of the neighbourhood, was the brother of the secretary of the Commission, who, in his turn, was a man of education and of keen intelligence. It seemed hardly probable, having regard to this relationship, that the farmer would come forward to accuse his landlord of a criminal offence without preliminary conversation with his brother at the Bar. The accusation, in fact, bore every mark of careful preparation, and there need be no hesitation in saying that the party which alleged intimidation to prevail, which asserted that the pretended terror of the tenantry rested upon substantial grounds, looked upon Mr. John Thomas with the same confidence which a whist-player reposes in the king of trumps. Mr. Watkins, however, came forward to reply. He was warned, as prisoners are supposed to be warned by the arresting constable that any admissions made by them may be used against them later, that he was under no compulsion to make his defence. But, albeit harassed a good deal from the Bench, he was not daunted, and he gave his explanation. He was perhaps wise not to rely on the defence that the original statements of his accuser had not been marked by *bonâ fides*. True it is that the statements were irritating and that he had denied them. But the questions whether rents are too high, whether an agent is competent, whether favouritism is shown, and who has the right in a petty squabble about a rabbit warren, were questions on which Mr. John Thomas had a right to an opinion. But besides this, Mr. Watkins had an explanation, amply sufficient if it were true, which Mr. John Thomas did not attempt to deny comprehensively. Mr. Thomas, said Mr. Watkins, was always grumbling, and, prior to the giving of his evidence, it had been agreed verbally that he should quit his farm on the following 29th of September. This verbal agreement he did not fulfil; verbal agreements of that kind seldom are fulfilled. Mr. Watkins was accordingly instructed to give him formal notice at the next opportunity, which was, of course, the next 29th of September ; and he gave it. So Mr. Watkins played the ace of trumps to the agitator's king.

Such was the version of the transaction given by Mr. Watkins, a gentleman whose position and reputation entitled him to credit. Nor, substantially, was it denied by Mr. John Thomas. In truth, it was quite possible that both views of the affair might be correct, Mr. Watkins on his part holding it to be his duty to carry out his instructions in the proper course, while Mr. John Thomas, very likely felt that the whole thing had blown over. Some of the questions asked of Mr. Watkins by individual Commissioners have an incidental interest as an exemplification of the mood in which they approached questions between landowner and tenant. Why, it was asked, was not Mr. Thomas informed immediately on his failure to quit the holding as agreed, that notice would be given to him formally at the next proper opportunity ? The answer, of course, is plain. A warning of this kind would have amounted to giving Mr. Thomas nearly two years' notice to quit. To have given so much notice would have been to expose Mr. Thomas to a considerable temptation, for, as every farmer knows, it is easy in the course of two years to transmute much of the inherent richness of a farm into cash. " Mr. Watkins is not," says Mr. Thomas, " a practical farmer" ; but he seems to have known this elementary rule of estate management.

So far we have seen the Commission, after professing to see that it had no business to express an opinion as to the criminality of conduct, pronouncing a solemn condemnation of two gentlemen. Was this condemnation uttered of set purpose or, so to speak, by accident? If of set purpose, then it is difficult to acquit of hypocrisy the man or men responsible for the original sentence ; if by accident, it can only be said that the error was of a singularly clumsy character.

The dilemma is one in which we are quite satisfied that the Commissioners should be left; they are entitled to impale themselves on the horn of their choice.

Fortunately final judgment upon the question whether a number of Welsh landowners had rendered themselves obnoxious to the criminal law did not lie with Lord Carrington and his associates. They might listen to wild accusations, supported by statements which could never be accepted as evidence in a criminal court; they might hector the accused after hearing as much, or as little, as they pleased of the case for the defence; they might tickle the ears of the groundlings by vague talk of the Public Prosecutor. And, no doubt, it was not pleasant for the gentlemen against whom charges affecting their honour, and even their liberty, were made, to feel that their cases were being considered by the Solicitor to the Treasury. But the result was satisfactory, for that official, being compelled both by legal and moral duty to give impartial consideration to the statements submitted to him, reported of each case that the statements made would not justify a prosecution. In other words, the Commission had recommended not one but several gentlemen to the tender mercies of the Public Prosecutor, and the cold-blooded official had, by his action if not by his words, condemned the whole series of charges as trumpery and unsubstantial. What, in those circumstances, was the plain duty of the Commissioners? Surely, although every lawyer familiar with the facts, with the solitary exception of the Queen's Counsel who stood for law on the Commission, had laughed to scorn the menace of prosecution, common humanity and decency pointed to the only course worthy of honourable men. They had dangled fine and imprisonment before the eyes of responsible gentlemen, themselves, for the most part, entrusted with the duty of administering justice. They had been informed, on high authority, that they had threatened in vain and without reason, that out of many reckless accusa-

tions there was not a single one which could be brought
forward, either in a Court of summary jurisdiction or before
a jury, with the slightest prospect of obtaining a conviction.
From private gentlemen who had fallen publicly into so
gross and calumnious a blunder, an ample apology would
have been demanded by public opinion. But officials, how-
soever ephemeral, must not sully their dignity by confession
of error. At least, however, the official mind might have
remembered that it was neither humane nor necessary to
keep the threatened gentlemen in suspense. Yet it is a
plain fact that, until November 1896, when the Commission,
under the spur of the just remonstrance of the Treasury, was
forced to produce its voluminous Report, no official information, no intimation that they might take their walks abroad
in peace of mind, was vouchsafed to these gentlemen who lay
under menace.

For this extraordinary silence there was, it is plain from
the Report, a similar reason. The majority of the Commissioners ought, in all charity, to have been pleased to find that
skilled investigation had shown their suspicions to be groundless; but their conduct shows plainly that their feelings were
of quite another character. It is the literal fact that after
the Solicitor to the Treasury had reported that in no case
could a prosecution be instituted with the remotest prospect
of success, a deputation of the Commissioners actually had
the hardihood to wait upon the Home Secretary to urge, in
malignant despair, prosecution in spite of the Solicitor to the
Treasury. The deputation, we learn from the Report, consisted of Lord Carrington and Mr. Brynmor Jones, Q.C., M.P. ;
and the deputation was, as Mr. Kenelm Digby's letter
proves, answered with dignity and with courtesy, in which the
tone of reproof is distinctly to be traced.

Finally the Commissioners, or some of them, for we decline
to assume that any individual Commissioner can be responsible for the form of every sentence in this huge volume, return

to the charge in their Report. They condemn the very persons whom the Public Prosecutor has declared that no jury could possibly condemn, they whine that the Act of Parliament is inadequate, because, forsooth, it requires that no man shall be punished until his guilt has been established by evidence.

No apology need be offered for the careful treatment which has been given to this subject. It has been given not so much in jealousy for the reputation of South Wales and Monmouthshire landowners, which in truth stands too high to be affected by groundless and pertinacious calumny, as in the feeling that the subject itself is of vital importance in relation to every proposal for agrarian legislation. This allegation of fear, this assertion that the peasantry of Wales are so terror-stricken and so timorous by constitution and tradition that they are not free agents in the affairs of life and not capable of looking after their own business, is at the bottom of the whole of the reactionary and unscientific proposal for the establishment of a system of judicial rents. Before the Commission started upon its pilgrimage the vernacular Press imagined this fear and invented it to be an excuse for a poor and unprovable case. The Commissioners have accepted this theory of fear and have made it the foundation of their Report. The party of agitation have strained themselves to the utmost to discover so much as a scintilla of evidence tending to show that facts supported their stolid assertion that the tenantry stand in terror of the landowners. In truth, the party of agitation looked beyond the Commission and saw that, before their confiscatory designs could hope to receive the serious attention of the House of Commons, they must produce something approaching to evidence to show that their stories were true. The mere assertion that an entire race lived in groundless and unreasoning terror was one at which the country and the House of Commons would not look in a serious mood. It is, therefore, a matter of grave importance and satisfaction that, after exercising all their energies, after using every device which malice and ingenuity could suggest, these persons have failed signally to produce a particle of foundation for the alleged fear, or a single *primâ facie* case of intimidation of a witness or injury done to a witness by reason of evidence, true or false, given by him.   The only kind of intimidation which existed in connection with the Welsh Land Commission came from the Bench and was applied to witnesses who had the hardihood to disagree with the views, we will not call them principles, as to the tenure of land held by six out of the nine Commissioners, and by, perhaps, one Englishman out of twenty.

CHAPTER III

From the allegation of national terror, which is at once an insult to the Welsh people and a condemnation of Welsh landowners as a body, the Commissioners proceed to condemn Welsh land and estate agents as a body. The condemnation is pronounced inferentially in the first two recommendations of the Commissioners, which have been compared, unkindly but most justly, to copy-book precepts. The Commissioners recommend estate owners to be careful in the choice of their agents, to choose Welsh-speaking agents for Welsh-speaking districts, to see that their agents are properly qualified. They urge agents to organise themselves into a profession, to be impartial in their treatment of tenants and, oddly enough, never to act upon the testimony of their subordinates.

All this is, of course, on the face of it, mere petty trifling; but unhappily the mere fact that nine gentlemen, after three years of travel at the expense of the taxpayer, deem it necessary to advise Welsh landowners to follow the obvious dictates of common sense, compels an inference. That inference is that landowners have not been careful in the choice of agents; that agents are, as a body, not competent, and not impartial. Nor are we left to inference only, for on p. 251 of the Report is found the following passage:

"We cannot wholly acquit all the owners of Wales in the past or in the present of having employed improper or in some cases unprincipled persons as agents, or having with scanty or too slight inquiry and examination acquiesced in and obtained advantage from harsh, arbitrary, and ill-advised proceedings." This sentence is qualified and watered down a little, but the whole is calculated to leave the impression that the Commissioners, or so many of them as endorsed this sentence, have a very poor opinion of the quality of Welsh estate agents.

It is necessary to say one word by way of preliminary to our defence of agents against a condemnation which has really no substantial foundation. That is that, when we speak of agents we refer to persons who manage considerable estates, and not to mere rent collectors of isolated farms, who may be bankers, or accountants, or lawyers, or even, as in one case, confectioners. It is ridiculous to speak of such persons as agents, and absurd to suppose that the small properties of which they collect the rents could support the expense of a professional and trained agent. Moreover, the tenants on such properties must be and are perfectly well aware that the relation between them and the owners is purely contractual. They may be better or they may be worse off than tenants on large estates, for on some small estates much money is expended by the owners; but the men who collect the rents are not, in any true sense of the word, agents.

A very large part of the arable and pastoral area of Wales is, however, under the management of agents, and we are concerned to defend them against a rambling condemnation, the injustice of which has been very generally felt. That becomes the easier in that the Commissioners have favoured the world with a species of summary of the evidence on which they rely, and a study of that summary is instructive, since it shows the Commissioners to have been influenced by general and wholly valueless allegations, unsupported by specific facts and in revolt against the despotism of facts. The summary too is in many cases unfair and misleading by reason of omission of material facts. A brief treatment of the summary of evidence so far as it relates to South Wales and Monmouthshire will exemplify our meaning.

It is quite true that Mr. Edward John of Cowbridge, who is a tradesman, said "The appointment of inexperienced agents has been most detrimental to the best interests of both landlord and tenants." But he gave no instances and, as a plain matter of fact, he was speaking in the hearing of the principal agents of Glamorganshire, of whom the great majority have enjoyed special training. To suggest, for example, that such men as Mr. Knox, Miss Talbot's agent, and Mr. Forrest, Lord Windsor's agent, or Mr. Randall, Lord Dunraven's agent, were not competent, would be simply childish. Again, Mr. John Williams, speaking of the same county, said: "Agents had generally had no practical training." But this was a ranting witness, who went on to say at once: "There are Scotchmen coming down here, and they do not know anything," which is not, perhaps, the general experience, which is that Scotchmen often know too much. Contrast this loose kind of statement with the deliberate evidence of Mr. Herbert Lloyd, who, speaking of Western Glamorganshire, said that "all the agents he knew, and he knew them all in that district, were men of great practical experience, and fair men too, and who did their best to see that justice was done to the tenants." This is the language of a man who knew what he was talking about; and he was not cross-examined on the subject from the body of the room or from the bench. Then, we are told, "Mr. W. Jenkins, of Rhoose Farm, near Barry, complained of mismanagement by agents, and especially instanced the case of an agent who was brother-in-law of the landlord and of the rector of the parish," and some quite general abuse of agents is appended. The general abuse does not matter, but the first specific mention of mismanagement seems worthy of investigation. Will it be believed that the action, thus roughly described as "mismanagement," consisted simply and entirely in raising a rent in the prosperous times of 1875, a process which is far more likely to have been good management than bad? Next comes a series of passages relating to North Wales, and then we are regaled with the views of Mr. W. Gibbs of Pembroke-shire, as to the qualifications which agents ought to possess; Mr. Gibbs, however, is not quoted as denying that agents may possess these qualifications. The Commissioners more-over add, in justice, that Major Wynne, one of the principal agents of the district for which Mr. Gibbs spoke, has had practical training at Downton, and at an architect's office. Mr. Moses Williams (Carmarthenshire) then complained that Sir Arthur Stepney's agent could not talk Welsh, which is true. But Mr. Wilson knows his business as well as any man in Wales or in England, and while the advantage of Welsh-speaking in agents is not denied, it is plain that it may be exaggerated and that the ignorance of English pretended by Cymric enthusiasts is also greatly exaggerated. Few indeed are the farmers, even in the remotest parts of Wales, who cannot go through a commercial bargain in English and keep remarkably level with, if not ahead of, the monoglot English-men.

Then comes a new kind of indictment from the mouth of Mr. Llewelyn Williams, in which no complaint is made of agents, but in which it is said that many landowners listen to intermediaries in the nature of spies and tale-bearers. No particular instances are quoted, so that the statement is of little or no value; but in any case it does not affect the character of agents individually, or as a body. Next, Mr. John Thomas, Llandilo, was permitted to say "too often the agent is a solicitor, or bank-clerk, or auctioneer, who knows little of the importance and responsibility of his office." This statement, although untrustworthy in its want of specific reference, calls for some comment. We may pass over the bank-clerk; he is a mere rent collector, but it really is not very uncommon for solicitors to be agents, or for agents to be solicitors, or for auctioneers to be agents. Now, the Commissioners and some of the witnesses made a dead set at solicitors, and it is rather difficult to see the rationale of their attitude. Knowledge of the law of landlord and tenant can hardly be reckoned a disadvantage ; and knowledge of the law does not exclude other knowledge. To be blunt, a country solicitor doing a little farming on his own account, familiar with the affairs and circumstances of his neighbours, accustomed to judge the characters of men, is quite competent to manage the business of any estate. In special cases he may, as Sir C. G. Philipps's solicitor-agent showed, call in an expert. He may not possess all the scientific knowledge which is at the command of the best agents of great estates ; but, after all, it is surely putting the claims upon a landowner rather high to insist that he shall provide for the men who hire his land a gratuitous tutor in agriculture. He may do it if he pleases, but it is not just to demand it of him as of right. Moreover, such a man is liable to be classed by malcontents of the type of Mr. Gwilym Evans, whose claim to authority rests mainly on his Quinine Bitters, among those agents " who have a rather high opinion of their own abilities as compared with those of tenant farmers." As for the auctioneers, there are no men who know the value of land and its capacities better. They are very often and very properly selected as agents, Mr. T. Rule Owen, of Haverfordwest, being a conspicuous and excellent example.

The complaint of Mr. Gwilym Evans concerning the agents of a single estate may be put down as whimsical. He observed that the landlord was a good deal out of the country, that in twenty years he had had four or five agents in succession, and that the various agents (none of whom were alleged to be untrained) differed in their views of farming. Now, as to absenteeism. Welsh landowners are not charged with it even by the majority of the Commissioners, and it is really a little difficult to see how, so long as the conditions of human life remain as they are, or until all men are cast in one mould, changes of agents are to be prevented. Agents are human. They are liable to be of many degrees of intelligence, of many characters; they may find that they have entered into the service of principals with whom they cannot continue to work, or that the climate of a district does not suit their tastes or their constitutions, or that an opportunity of improving their positions offers itself. Nor, for a moment, do we dream of saying that they are perfect to a man. But we do venture to say that such a complaint as that of Mr. Gwilym Evans is wholly unreasonable, and shows him and his party to have been very hard-driven for evidence. Next we read, " Mr. David W. J. Thomas, of Brecon, is an instance of an owner acting as his own agent, though he had no practical knowledge of farming." In strict English this sentence is meaningless; the proper thing for the Commissioners to say would have been " Mr. Thomas, although he is not a practical farmer, employs no agent." Clearly, therefore, no defects in Mr. Thomas can affect the question of competence in agents. But in common fairness it ought to have been added that Mr. Thomas owns but 1000 acres of land : and it would be unreasonable to suggest that it was his duty to employ a special agent for the management of an estate of that area.

Then Mr. David Davies alleged that the agents in the Llandovery districts were Churchmen and Conservatives and that the differences of religious and political opinion estranged landlord and tenant. We are not yet prepared to admit without argument that either Churchmanship or Conservatism imply incompetence, and the charges of religious favouritism failed everywhere. But the plain truth of the matter is that this is one of many charges against landowners and agents which broke down completely.

To continue this analysis to the tedious end would exhaust the reader. Let it suffice to say that from beginning to end of the evidence relating to the competence of agents in South

Wales, not a single specific instance was given which even tended to prove that tenants had suffered injustice from want of competence or want of honesty on the part of any individual agent during recent years. On the other hand, it was shown in numerous cases, although it was practically impossible to bring forward the testimony in every individual case, that taken as a body the real estate agents of South Wales and Monmouthshire were, and are, as competent and honest a body as can be found in any country.

The requirements of the Commission on this point strike the ordinary mind as overstrained and exaggerated in the highest and most absurd fashion. They have attempted to define the standard or typical agent. " We think that such a typical agent should be one who in addition to a sound, preliminary, general, and scientific education has received a special theoretical training in agriculture and land surveying, and in the sciences (such as mathematics, chemistry, &c.), upon the practice of which these arts depends, as well as practical experience in an estate office and on a farm. To put the matter in another way, we think a young man intending to become a land-agent should, in addition to acquiring the average degree of culture and knowledge of a University man, attend courses of study at an agricultural college or a college giving technical instruction in the practical arts, and then pass some time gaining practical and actual experience in an office or a farm." After admitting that, until quite recently, the opportunities for producing these perfectly trained agents did not exist they say, "Most of those who are now agents in Wales never had the option of going through such a preliminary career." That is quite true ; the elder agents have every right to adopt the reply of the man who, on being accused of having been born in a poorhouse, retorted, "How could I be born in a poorhouse where no poorhouse was ? " But they might have added in justice that the mass of the younger generation of considerable agents,

such men, for example, as Mr. Knox, agent for the Margam
estate, Mr. Cowper Coles, agent to the Duke of Beaufort and
Sir Joseph Bailey, Mr. Dudley Drummond, Mr. Mouseley the
younger, Major Wynne, and many more besides, have used
every opportunity provided by modern zeal for specialised
training.   For our part, we venture to say that these gentlemen, good agents as they are, one and all, are fully prepared
to admit, are indeed even anxious to protest, that they are by
no means anxious to be compared to their own advantage with
agents of the older school who have learned their business
from experience.   They would tell us also, no doubt, that
experience in the transaction of estate business, intercourse
with tenant farmers, knowledge of the world and of character
in general, and study of the individuals under their charge
have been of infinitely more value to them than their special
training.

Next, after speaking of the excellence of some of the
agents produced by the "loose and unsatisfactory training,"
the Commissioners go to say, "Taking the man produced by
that training as the typical agent, we have no hesitation in
saying that the majority of agents, particularly in the more
Welsh districts, fall below this high but proper standard."
Which standard? If the Commissioners mean that these
gentlemen were not trained in institutions which did not
exist when they were doing their best to train themselves,
the sentence is merely puerile. Yet it is difficult to extract
any other meaning from this pompous statement.

The next passage is so remarkably spiteful that we must
quote it in full:

" Many even of those who have had considerable experience,
and who are kind and just in their dealings with tenants fail
in point of knowledge. They are unable to advise tenant
farmers, or to suggest new, or correct old, methods of
farming. So, again, many of them have no real experience

what farming is, do not understand the tenant's difficulties, and therefore, often reject reasonable demands as unreasonable, and put down as a grumble what is a well-founded complaint. It is clear that some owners have, themselves, never rightly appreciated the importance of special training and experience as a qualification of the agent. From motives of kindness, or of friendship, or of economy, they have too often appointed relatives, retired officers, and poorer country gentlemen, who may have been competent to discharge the office and easier business, but who had little knowledge of actual farming, and who often shared the prejudices and possessed the views of the landlord class, unalloyed by the sobering influence of the responsibility and anxiety of ownership of a landed estate. We are not saying a single word against the appointment of a properly trained person simply because he is a relation of the owners, or has served her Majesty in the army. For instance, not a word is suggested against men like Mr. O. S. Wynne, Mr. Dudley Drummond, or Major Birch."

Be it remembered that we have gone through the evidence which the Commissioners have selected to justify their observations. We may assume, and in truth it is the fact, that they selected the cream of that evidence. We have found it to consist of wildly general allegations of incompetence, not tested in a single instance, and therefore clearly not to be relied upon. Equally clear is it that the Commissioners have relied upon it and upon nothing else. We say without hesitation that the opinion expressed is groundless and uncharitable. Moreover, we challenge the majority of the Commissioners, and particularly their representative in the House of Commons, to justify the sentence beginning, " From motives of kindness." Their summary of evidence contains but one instance of a relative appointed agent, in the shape of Commander Thomas. It is in evidence that he has enjoyed

D

special training. There is no evidence that he is poor, and there is evidence that the estate which he manages is in apple-pie order. He is, it is true, an ex-Commander of the Navy, and as such, he is one of two retired officers who are mentioned in the summary as agents. The other is Major Wynne, who again has special training. We protest, indignantly, and we venture to say with justice, that the majority of the Commissioners have been, to use a favourite word of Mr. Brynmor Jones, " hasty " and without warrant in making this accusation. It has no basis. It is not true.

And what is the inference to be drawn from the three names at the end, taken in connection with the preceding sentence, by persons not familiar with Welsh society, that is to say, by the persons to whom this Report is addressed ? It is that the three persons named are notable exceptions to the imaginary rule that poor and incompetent relatives and retired officers are appointed as agents. Mr. Drummond is no doubt the brother of Sir James Drummond; he is also his agent. It would have been just to add that he is also Lord Cawdor's agent. Major Birch is undoubtedly a retired officer who is a very good agent in North Wales. But he would be the first to protest that in this matter he is not singular. Mr. Owen Slaney Wynne is, no doubt, the agent of Mr. Wynne of Penarth, who is his brother; but he is not at all poor, he was agent for the Wynnstay estates for many years, and he has virtually spent his life in estate management. The sting of the sentence lies in the innuendo. The men who say nothing against Mr. Wynne, Mr. Drummond, and Major Birch clearly imply that, if they were not so kindly in disposition, if they were not so desperately afraid of hurting the sensibilities of men, they could say a great deal against others. That is not a fair or a generous proceeding.

It is true that the Commissioners end their summary of

so-called evidence with the words, " For obvious motives we
abstain from referring to the body of testimony we received
as to the qualifications, character, and merits of individual
agents." As a matter of fact, the sentence is not accurate, for
the summary contains references to the qualifications of several
agents. But we are at a loss to understand these "obvious
motives," for, to our mind, it is infinitely more unmanly to
condemn a whole class without citing a single specific example
than it would be to search among the volumes of evidence,
almost in vain, for cases of injustice or incompetence.

An examination of the evidence upon which the Commissioners have condemned agents proves clearly that the
condemnation is wholly without justification. It may be
added that the standard of excellence declared to be indis-
pensable, or "high and proper," is far too lofty. The matter
must be looked upon from a common-sense point of view,
and, by way of illustration, I will look at the conditions which
prevail in my own county of Carnarvon. There the estates of
Lord Penrhyn, Mr. Assheton Smith, Colonel Wynne Finch,
Mr. Nanney, and Mr. Wynn, and perhaps one or two more,
are sufficiently large to render the employment of first-rate
agents at handsome salaries possible. The agencies are all
occupied, and will, I trust, continue to be held by their
present occupants for many years to come. What young man
in his senses, having no special claims on any one of these
owners, is going to the expense of passing through all the
courses indicated by the Commissioners in the hope of obtaining any one of these agencies ? It is not, of course, denied
that, to a man otherwise well equipped to be an agent, these
acquirements may be very useful, but it is certain that other
parts of the proper equipment of an agent are of far greater
importance. An agent must be just, honourable, sympathetic,
careful of the interests of his principal, quick to discern
between the true and the false complaint. Moreover, it seems
to us, the Commissioners take far too magnificent a view of

the obligations of landowners. The legal relation of landlord
and tenant is contractual. The tenant takes so much land,
with so much capital of the owner's invested in it, on certain
terms. In law, if he takes on terms disadvantageous to
himself, he must suffer. In practice he does not, since there
is abundant evidence at the end of this volume to show that
landowners are in a large measure philanthropical institutions.
From humanity of feeling, from affection for their tenantry,
from pride in their estates, they perform acts of generosity
outside the contract, and relieve the tenant from many of his
obligations under the contract. But this is done of grace by
men who can afford it, not of compulsion. It is the kind of
obligation which clearly ought not to be enforced by law.
And how does this affect the question of agents? Surely
very closely. It is an excellent thing for the tenant to have
the opportunity of consulting an agent who is an expert in
agriculture ; it would be still better for the tenant if, say once
in a hundred cases, he took the advice given to him. But to
contend, as the majority of the Commissioners appear to
contend, that a landowner, however small, ought to provide
at his own expense an expert adviser for a tenant who ought
to know his own business is to carry things too far. Far be it
from us to regret the great services to Welsh agriculture
which owners of large areas of Welsh land, particularly those
enjoying an income from other sources than agricultural
land, have been able and willing to render. To them the
country is under a deep debt of obligation. But they would
certainly be the first to protest that, in so far as they have
been able to give more substantial help to their tenantry in
bad times than has been possible for their less wealthy
neighbours to offer, the difference has been due largely to the
fact of their superior wealth. It is a plain fact, unfortunately,
that no man can, for any length of time, give away money
which he does not possess. Similarly the man of small estate
cannot afford to employ a qualified and expert agent ; and

the man of large means can employ such an agent. So much, in the majority of cases, tho better for the tenant on the large estate; but it would be the very absurdity of injustice to suggest the statutory enforcement upon small estates of the conditions, due mainly to generosity, which prevail upon great estates.

CHAPTER IV

A PRELIMINARY warning may well be uttered at the outset of this chapter, which is devoted in part to distinguishing the conditions of tenancy in South Wales and Monmouthshire, as elicited in the evidence given before Lord Carrington's Commission, from the conditions presumed by Parliament to exist in Ireland before the series of Land Acts beginning in 1860, added to periodically until 1896, and likely to be added to from year to year, was started.

Firstly, there is good reason to believe, as indeed Lord Ormathwaite's evidence before Lord Carrington suggested, that the Irish landowners as a body were never quite so bad as they were said to be, and that, if proper steps had been taken to place their case before the country, it might have been shown that they, like their colleagues in Wales and in England, had invested very considerable sums in their estates for the mutual benefit of themselves, as they fondly hoped, and of their tenants. Secondly, it must not be taken to be admitted here that, even if the party of agitation had been able to show that the so-called Irish conditions existed in Wales, there would be a sufficient justification for the introduction into Wales of the present Irish system, or chaos, or of any part of it. In Ireland itself so much evil has been wrought by successive, confiscatory, and contradictory statutes, that it will probably be necessary to go on tinkering away at the so-called Irish system for ever. Landowners will not invest money in buildings and improvements,

because they know full well that the law and the Land
Courts between them will absolutely forbid them to see any
of the interest of their money. These gentlemen, among
them being one noted for his generosity in South Wales, say
plainly that before the legislation they spent money on their
estates, but that since the legislation they have spent none.
Why should they, when successive Acts of Parliament have
reduced them from affluence to straitened means, and in
some cases to absolute poverty ? Similarly the tenant's right
of free sale, which had a historical meaning in Ulster, but
none outside Ulster, seemed at the outset a great boon to the
tenantry. So much was sliced away from what the landlord
had to sell or to let on hire, and given to the tenant to sell in
the open market if he chose. In hundreds and thousands of
cases the sitting tenant has sold at auction prices, and the
result, which the most ardent supporter of the Irish Land
Laws does not attempt to deny, is that hundreds and
thousands of the Irish tenantry are holding their land, for all
practical purposes, subject to a yearly charge which it is
practically impossible for them to pay. This charge is not
the judicial rent ; that, indeed, is already reduced almost to
vanishing point, but the interest on the money which the in-
coming tenant must borrow to pay the outgoing tenant for
the statutory right of occupation.

No; the state of the Irish tenantry, the extravagant prices
that have been paid for tenant-right, and the continual calls
made upon Parliament for new measures to alleviate the
evils created by statute, are and must remain for all reasonable persons an absolute argument against all proposals to
introduce the Irish system or no-system into Wales or into
England. That, if such a system is introduced into Wales, it
must also invade England, is quite obvious—but that is by
the way.

It is plain, however, that there are two positions from
which this question may be approached, and it is therefore

prudent, without adopting our opponents' point of view, or assenting to it, to see how the Welsh case looks from their standpoint; to say, in effect, " You look at the matter wrong-headedly, what you wish to enact could never, under any circumstances, be beneficial ; but we will do our best to show you that the facts are, even from your point of view, insufficient to justify the course which you would like to follow."

Now, what were the facts alleged against the landlords of Ireland ?   The main counts of indictment against them were (1) that they were habitual absentees, living in England or in foreign countries, and spending, far away from Ireland, the money which they received from the tenantry ; (2) that they, as a body, spent no money at all in the improvement or maintenance of their estates, and that consequently each increase of rent represented taxation of the tenant in respect of work done and money spent by him ; (3) that by eviction they absolutely confiscated the tenants' improvements.

We need not pause to inquire into the veracity of these allegations, which is fortunate, since the history of the Irish Land Question is at least as long and as intricate as it is interesting.   It suffices that nothing of the kind has been proved, or nearly proved, in the case of South Wales and Monmouthshire, or for that matter in the case of North Wales either.   Nay more, the contrary has been established.

Absenteeism.—The vice of absenteeism simply does not exist.   For this we have the word, or rather the multitudinous words, of the Commissioners.   " Between complete absentee-ism, of which Irish landlords . . . (here they are condemned root and branch) have, unfortunately, too often. in the past, afforded disastrous examples, and the practically continuous residence of the Welsh squire, whose means do not permit him the luxury of a London house, there are many degrees of absenteeism."   Again, "We have, however, no doubt that complete absenteeism is comparatively rare in Wales, in regard to estates of such a size as to afford sufficient income to maintain a family comfortably. In fact, we are inclined to think that in proportion to their numbers a larger proportion of the Welsh landowners reside all, or nearly all the year on their estate, than is the case in any corresponding area in England." This seems a little unkind to the English land-owners, concerning whom the Welsh members of the Com-mission, with the exceptions of Lord Kenyon and Sir John Llewelyn, are not likely to have possessed any special know-ledge. But it is enough for our purposes to know that Welsh landowners are not condemned of absenteeism. Finally, it is somewhat amusing to note the manner in which the Commissioners arrive at a conclusion in the case of Glamorganshire. It is a county "in regard to which the charge of an undue amount of absenteeism might *à priori* be expected to be proved. . . . As a whole, the county is, therefore, not one that presents very great attractions to a landowner of sporting tastes, or even simply anxious for the peace of country life after a session of Parliament or a London season. It may, therefore, be taken as a test case without unfairness to those who complain of absenteeism." The simplicity of the last sentence is remarkable. The county best qualified, in the opinion of the Commissioners, to encourage absenteeism, is chosen as a test case " without un-fairness to those who complain of absenteeism." But what about those who assert, as we do, and as the Commissioners are compelled to admit, that absenteeism is practically un-known ? Is the test case fair to them ? Well, it does not much matter ; for on the basis of the Glamorganshire figures the Commissioners come to the conclusion that not more than five per cent. of the owners of a thousand acres and more can be described as absentees. Congratulation is due to the Commissioners also upon the fact that they have recognised the futility of talking of absenteeism in the case of smaller owners. A tenant has been heard to complain that his land-

lord was an absentee when the only land owned by the landlord was the tenant's holding. If that landlord had not been
an absentee there could have been no tenant.

Welsh landowners, therefore, are not absentees. A Commission so constituted as to be unfavourable to them in
the proportion of two to one has formally acquitted them
of a charge which has frequently been brought against
them.

Next comes the very important question whether it is true,
as alleged by the party of agitation in the House of Commons
and in print, that the agricultural improvements of Wales
are, as a rule, to be regarded as the fruit of the labour and
the expenditure of the tenants; or whether the landowners,
as a body, can be said to have done their share, and to be, so
to speak, partners with the tenantry.

It is obvious that generalisations on this question are
dangerous, and that to attempt to establish a precise rule
must be misleading. The custom of different counties
varies, the custom of different estates varies, the custom
of the same estate varies under successive owners. Before
arriving at any just conclusion it is necessary in each case to
consider all the incidents of the bargain between landlord
and tenant.

Here are a few examples. There is an estate in North
Wales on which a system of improving leases prevailed par-
tially for some time. That is to say, the tenant was allowed
to hold the land at a nominal rent for a term of years on
condition that he made certain improvements, and the said
improvements, at the end of the term, became the property
of the landlord. In Anglesey, again, the prevailing, but not
the universal, practice is for the landlord to supply the raw
material for structural improvements and for the tenant to
supply the labour. The same custom, by the way, prevails
on one of the largest estates in Hertfordshire. So, on the
Margam estate, the practice (as shown by the evidence of

Mr. Knox, the agent, Q. 25964) has varied. The habit of the late Mr. Talbot was to cast upon the tenants the duty of "repairs." "They had to do the repairs themselves, and Mr. Talbot's practice was to reduce the rent 10 per cent., so that the tenants should do the repairs." That policy has been reversed by Miss Talbot, under the advice of Mr. Knox, who is of opinion that the old policy was not beneficial to landlord or tenant; and under Miss Talbot "everything is put into repair, the buildings, fences, gates and everything, and materials are supplied for repairs." Yet another point may be mentioned concerning this estate with a view to show the danger of generalisation.

"Is it," said the Chairman (25968), "considered a high-rented or low-rented estate?"

"I think, as a rule, my lord, that the Margam estate is considered low-rented. I may say that the County Council two years ago were dissatisfied with the valuation of Margam parish, and they appointed a gentleman to value it, who had been a tenant-farmer. I am sorry to say that he died two or three months ago. The result of his valuation was that out of 107 holdings in Margam parish, 62 are held at rents *below the gross estimated rental put by this gentleman*, 29 are held at rents equal to the gross estimated rental, and only 16 are above the gross estimated rental." Again, "the rent is the same as when the tenant was under covenant to repair."

This striking case illustrates forcibly the misleading tendency of all generalisation. The estate, like many others, is low-rented. The tenants, under Mr. Talbot, accepted the 10 per cent. reduction on a low rental, and did not perform their contracts to repair. Miss Talbot came in, reversed Mr. Talbot's policy, and spent £31,000 in three years, besides giving abatements in bad years. The case is, as we have said, striking, but there are numerous other cases, presenting

many variations of practice, which tend to show that to
establish a general rule is quite impossible.

It was considered expedient, during the sittings of the
Commission, that landowners and agents in giving evidence
should state the expenditure upon buildings and improvements by them on the estates with which they were connected,
but it is not really to the purpose to quote those figures at
length. It is enough to say that the sums shown to have
been spent were strikingly large, and that they disposed
effectually of the suggestion that the presumption was that
the mass of the improvements, the greater part of the
difference between prairie value and present value, was due
to the exertions and expenditure of tenants. So large were
the figures, so well were they supported by reference to
estate accounts, that we may safely challenge the most hardy
of agrarian agitators to repeat the ancient theory that the
tenants were the improvers, or that the landlords have confiscated the fruits of their labour. Farther than this we have
no desire to go; indeed, to go farther would be illogical,
inconsistent with the principle laid down (that all the
incidents of a tenancy must be considered simultaneously),
and ignorant. Comparisons such as the Commissioners, and
some witnesses, strove to institute are not only odious but
also misleading. There is no reason why the tenant should
not undertake, or why he should not be compelled to perform,
a covenant to repair, if his rent is at such a standard as to
make the bargain fair. There is no moral difference between
the owner who manages his estate on that principle and the
owner who prefers to make sure and to do the repairs
himself. Manifestly, assuming three estates to be of equal
quality, the owner who does all the improvements and repairs
is entitled to exact a higher rent per acre than the owner
who supplies materials only; and he again is entitled to
exact a higher rent than the man who casts the whole duty
upon the tenants. Each and all of the bargains is equally

legitimate. It follows that to compare the expenditure of the first-named (and most usual) type of landowner with that of the second or the third type is a very ignorant proceeding.

Still, the unscientific mind is greatly impressed by large figures, and for this reason it was deemed prudent to place before the Commission the expenditure of a number of owners, an expenditure only accompanied in the rarest cases by a charge in the nature of interest. So far as they go these figures tend to establish the presumption that permanent improvements are the work of landowners, and there is virtually no definite testimony in the other direction. True it is, of course, that rents have risen generally and very largely during the last two or three centuries; true it is also that individual witnesses have complained of rents raised in the days of their fathers and of their grandfathers solely on the basis of tenants' improvements. Usually these witnesses asserted that "the landlord never spent a penny on repairs or improvements"; but the plain truth of the matter is that these witnesses were as free from the knowledge which would have justified this statement. as they were from the fear of contradiction by men and women who were long ago in their graves. Moreover, in not a single case were witnesses reminded by the Commissioners that other circumstances, the development of railways for example and the growth of magnificent markets in the populous parts of South Wales, added a value to the land for which the tenants were in no way responsible. This consideration was laid before Mr. Thomas Ellis, M.P., at Bala, and Mr. Ellis in the opinion of the majority of the Commissioners, pulverised his interrogator. Let the passage in the Report speak for itself.

"Mr. J. E. Vincent, in a question which he put through us to Mr. T. E. Ellis, asked whether the latter would admit, in tracing some rents from dates at the end of the last century, that the value of land had increased since those dates by

reason of improved communication, a view to which Mr. Ellis
replied, 'Certainly, though under what law all the enhanced
value arising from improvement in the communication should
go to the rent-receiver, and not to the rent-producer, passes
my understanding.' " Fortunately the alleged limits of the
understanding of Mr. Ellis are not the beginning and end of
the whole matter ; and, as a matter of law and fact, the
reasoning which inspired the question is not at all difficult to
follow.

Once, in theory, the landowner was tenant in fee and the
Crown was the owner. Advancing civilisation soon put a
practical end to that theory, and now, for all practical
purposes, the tenant in fee is the true owner. Certainly no
law exists by which the Crown or the State can get rid of
him, unless he fails to pay his debts. Then his landed estate
may be sold, in which case another owner or owners will
step into his position. But essentially and, to a great extent
in practice, he is a permanent institution. The land is his,
and his legal right is to let it out on hire to whomsoever he
pleases, or to keep it in his own hands if he is so disposed.
On the other hand the tenant is theoretically. and to a large
extent in practice, a temporary institution. All the laws
enacted in his interest regard him in that light ; and although,
in a very large number of interesting cases, succession in
tenancy has been shown to be almost hereditary in families,
that succession in families has been accorded of grace, not
out of compulsion.

So much Mr. Ellis was presumed to know. It might
perhaps have been hoped that he would perceive that the
question was asked of him.

1. By way of discounting the suggestion that rents had
been raised upon tenants' improvements.

2. That if the improved communications of the end of this
century rendered the lot of the farmer to-day more tolerable
than the lot of the farmer at the end of the last century, it

was no particular hardship that he should pay more for the hire of the land than his predecessor of a century ago.

But it is plain that the majority of the Commissioners have not been able to bring themselves to say that the presumption in Wales is, as it is by law and is wrongly supposed to be in fact across the Irish Channel, that the improvements are the work of the tenants. The Report does not make this admission in the kindliest or most generous manner, but the admission is plainly present. " The individual landowners who have come before us have. it is plain, not been actuated by the sole desire of getting as much profit, or, to express it in a concrete term, as much money as they could out of their estates; they have in making expenditure upon them, in erecting new buildings or repairing old ones, been actuated by several motives. They have felt that ' property had its duties as well as its rights '; they have experienced *some feeling of compunction* at the wretched lives their tenants led in insanitary and inadequate houses; they have found a natural satisfaction in beautifying their estates, or at any rate in making the buildings compact and modern, in improving their property and giving to it a trim, neat, and ' model ' appearance. Most of them have become possessed of the estate on the death of a relation (generally near) and found the estate a going concern, *with the management of which they found it difficult to interfere without raising complications which would add to the troubles of life, and so have blindly and apathetically acquiesced in a method which has become traditional. Few, if any, have sat down and examined the situation* ab initio, *or exhaustively considered the first principles on which they should carry on the business of landowning. They have been the obedient followers of the family solicitor and the family agent. They have without independent investigation upon their stepping into the places of their predecessors, allowed things to take their course.* The improvement of the estate, meaning by that the erection of new buildings of better plan and the repair of old buildings, fences, roads, &c. (and in many cases, drainage) has been held out as a desirable object" (page 265).

The majority of the Commissioners, it is clear, have found themselves entirely unable to deny the plain fact that Welsh landowners are greatly devoted to the improvement of their estates. The evidence was too much for them; but, as the passages in italics (which are ours) show plainly, they did not hesitate to qualify their reluctant acquittal of the landowners by ascribing to them motives of which there was no evidence whatsoever. Now it happens that in South Wales very few landowners appeared before the Commission at all, and this for two reasons. Firstly, it was felt that agents would be more familiar with the facts and figures with which the Commission was presumably desirous of making acquaintance; secondly, the methods of cross-examination followed by the Commission were not such as to encourage those who ventured to differ from the Commission. Certainly the present writer advised on several occasions that the agent would be the better witness and, to be plain, would stand bullying better. But those who did come forward to give positive evidence, as distinct from mere rebuttal of false or one-sided accusations, certainly cannot be put down as blind or apathetic followers of any solicitor or agent. The writer quotes from memory only. In Glamorganshire, so far as his memory serves him, only one considerable landowner gave evidence; in Breconshire, two, Mr. J. A. Doyle, of Pendarren, and Sir Joseph R. Bailey; in Monmouthshire none at all, for in truth Monmouthshire took no interest in the Commission; in Pembrokeshire, none; in Carmarthenshire, none; in Cardiganshire, none, unless Mr. Vaughan Davies, M.P., counts. Certainly all who did come forward were men who had given deep thought to the subject and the last men in the world to be led by the nose by any agent or by any solicitor. Lest it be said on behalf of the Commission that the reference in this ungenerous passage is to North Wales, it may be as well to state that the principal landowners

who gave evidence there were Lord Penrhyn, who dealt with
a special subject having no connection with estate management and is not a weak or pliable man; Lord Stanley of
Alderley, who gave the Commission to understand plainly and
in detail, that he had very definite ideas of estate management; Mr. Ellis Nanney, who has devoted almost all his life
to the management of his estate; Mr. William Wynne, of
Peniarth, who showed himself closely familiar with estate
management; Mr. R. Lloyd Price, of Rhiwlas, who certainly
proved that he knew his business; and Mr. Edward Davies,
of Llandinan, who by his masterly evidence caused confusion
among the majority of the Commissioners, one of whom was
his own tenant. In fact, looking back at the evidence given
by landowners, it is impossible to say anything less severe
than that the whole of this statement which is italicised is
absolutely without warrant or foundation in the evidence
given by landowners before the Commission or in their
demeanour when giving it.

A curious passage follows: "Such, then, is the consistent
and logical interpretation of the economic position of the
landowner following the modern system of estate management as disclosed in the evidence. It may safely be asserted
that this system is followed in theory by nearly all the estate
owners in Wales." If this passage means anything—and
there is always a doubt whether the draughtsman of the
Report had any definite idea in his mind when he stumbled
on the fatal word "economic"—it means that the landowners
of Wales carry on a business, for the most part without
realising it; that in carrying on that business they are not
actuated by purely commercial motives; that they do improve
their estates for other reasons; and that they do it because
they are blind and apathetic and completely in the hands of
their men of business. There is a good deal of nonsense in
the passage, of course, but it is immaterial to our purpose,
for the question for the moment is not why landlords spend

E

money on their estates, but whether they do spend it; and
the Commissioners go on to confess this in so many words:
"Of course, some expend a much larger proportion of the
revenues in improving the estate than others; the ratio of the
capital so put into the business to the total capitalised value
of the estate in the market [of which the Commissioners had
no evidence at all, and which no one of them could pretend
to be competent to judge] is very different in different cases.
*But practically every owner has done something, has spent some
portion of his annual revenue, in improving his estate.*"

So at last, from the reluctant lips of an openly hostile
tribunal, is forced the admission that the main argument
used to justify the establishment of Land Courts in Ireland
cannot be used with any truth in the case of Wales.

But the Commissioners are driven harder than this. They
bestir themselves to attack the statement of Colonel Hughes,
the Wynnstay agent, that "the rent is only a moderate
interest upon the amount of the owner's money that has been
expended on the land and its maintenance." The Wynnstay
estate is almost, but not entirely, situate in North Wales, but
no other estate is so fully treated, and an examination of
the conclusions reached by the Commissioners will serve to
show alike their method of going to work and the large
extent of the confession of landlords' expenditure which they
have found themselves compelled to make. Colonel Hughes
was able to show that out of a gross rental of £1,425,454
collected in thirty-two years, no less than £295,233 had been
expended in purely agricultural repairs. To escape cavilling
criticism, it may be well to add that these all came under the
headings "Fencing, Gates, Wood," "Building and Repairs,"
and "Draining." The Commissioners frankly recognise that
further deductions from the gross rental might fairly be
made, and ought to be made, in respect of expenses of
management, which, in the case of an estate of more than
137,000 acres, spread over five counties, and in parts wild

and inaccessible, cannot fail to be very large. They notice also that temporary abatements of rent are not taken into consideration, and that no deduction has been made in respect of taxes or premiums for insurance. The present gross rental (1893) was stated at £13,548.

Now the Commission, after a philosophical discourse on the nature of interest, which was unnecessary, since all the world knows that interest is what men have to pay for the use of other men's money, work out the capitalised value of the buildings on the Wynnstay estate at £400,000 or £500,000. It does not concern us that this estimate is ridiculously small and that the grounds on which it is based are of the vaguest description. It is enough that they adjudge that the owner of the Wynnstay estate gets, at the most, 6 or 5 per cent. for his money. This they apparently think is too much; and they institute comparisons with consols and the dividends upon railway stock of the gilt-edged quality, and declare that a man can wish for no safer investment than that of his own money upon his own land. But they forget many things. First, that the owner has, on their own admission, to put aside at least 20 per cent. of his dividend to the maintenance of the security; secondly, that the expenses of management and collection are necessarily great; thirdly, that they themselves, by proposing to establish a Land Court, suggest that the value of the security, and its safety at the reduced value, ought to be greatly reduced.

Colonel Hughes, in short, has established his point, which is, that the landlord's profits or interest are but a moderate interest upon his investment. In practice 2 to 2½ per cent. at the most, minus abatements, represent the average interest obtained on investments in the purchase of agricultural land in South Wales and Monmouthshire. For the case of the Wynnstay estate is by no means singular. Mr. Talbot spent his money, that is to say, remitted his 10 per cent. and lost it; Miss Talbot has spent an enormous sum, and will have to spend much more. To continue other cases quoted by the Commissioners, Lord Dunraven has spent £58,000 on a rental of £10,000 in twenty-one years, or 27½ per cent. of the *gross* rental. Mr. Lort Phillips has spent 16·6 per cent. of his income in the same way; Lord Llangattock 10 to 15 per cent.; the Caerleon Charity 36 per cent; Lord Dynevor 18 per cent.; Mr. Picton Evans (one of the despised solicitors), on various Cardiganshire estates, 28, 7, and 7½ per cent.; Mr. J. C. Harford 33 per cent.; Lord Lisburne 20 per cent.; Lord Ormathwaite 25 per cent. These are the cases which the Commission deem it worth while to mention in South Wales and Monmouthshire. Others might be added, but it would not be to our purpose, which is not to prove, since the Commission have done that already, but to point out that, in a futile attack on the impregnable argument of Colonel Hughes, the Commission have succeeded in shattering the main plank of the platform upon which the proposal for a Land Court rests. It is the plain fact, admitted by them directly and indirectly, that the great mass of the permanent improvements, the buildings, the walls, the fences, the drains, are the fruit of the landlord's money, and are not to be credited to the tenant when a balance is struck between the parties. And that is all we desire to establish.

CHAPTER V.

THE next and most serious accusation made against land-owners is that they take advantage of an alleged Celtic passion for land, commonly called land-hunger, for the purpose of exacting from the tenantry rents higher than the condition of agriculture justifies.

First, let us speak of the so-called land-hunger. It is not to be denied that no farms in Wales, North or South, are derelict, as unhappily farms in purely arable parts of England are. Nor is there any doubt that when farms become vacant, particularly when they are of small area, so that an industrious man can enter upon them with the hope of succeeding, even though his capital be small, the number of applicants is large. Also the rents and capacities of all farms being perfectly well known in the neighbourhood in which they are situate, the number of applicants is usually greatest where the conditions of the farm offer the best hope of success. Land-hunger, if it exists, goes hand in hand with that keen eye for the main chance for which Welshmen have a well-merited reputation.

Numerous applications for vacant farms, however, are not necessarily evidence of the existence of land-hunger, which may be defined as so passionate a desire to occupy land that, under its influence, men will forget all considerations of prudence, and offer for the occupation of a farm more than is reasonable. Until the contrary is distinctly proved the obvious interpretation of the action of the farming class is to be preferred. When twenty men apply for a farm the obvious explanation of their action is that each and all of them think they can make a livelihood and a profit by earning it. Some of them may offer a higher rent than their neigbours. But they do it with perfect safety. They know perfectly well— this statement is made with full knowledge and deliberation —that there is not a single considerable estate in the whole of South Wales and Monmouthshire upon which the offers made by candidates for tenancy have the slightest influence in fixing the rent to be paid, and that both agents and land-lords are consistently animated by the desire to select as tenants those men who, by virtue of their intelligence, their industry, and their capital, are best calculated to do justice to the land and to themselves. Further, Welsh tenants have been described by competent authorities as the best rent-payers in the country.

So obvious is the inference to be drawn from each of these facts, that when the outcry against rents first made itself heard, the persons against whom the cry was raised replied, "There are plenty of applicants for farms, and the tenants pay their rents regularly." The inference left to be drawn was that the bargain between landlord and tenant was fair, and that the tenants had money. But the agitation-monger is as averse to the obvious, which is usually the true, interpretation of plain facts, as the sensational novelist is to the orderly sequence of events; so he suggested, as the explanation of facts which could not be denied, that the applicants for vacancies were proof positive of an overwhelming passion for land, peculiar to the Celtic nature, and for the last ten years or more he has been asserting that it was the regular practice for tenants to pay their rents with borrowed money. Now, this last assertion is, to be perfectly plain, arrant nonsense. Land-hunger there may or may not be, but it is commercially impossible that men should continue to pay their rents for ten years in succession with borrowed money. Of course a tenant may arrange with a banker for a temporary loan, to be repaid out of the proceeds of his sales of store stock at a forthcoming fair, or out of the price of his oats or barley. That is a mere matter of convenience; but to assert, as these men do, if they mean anything, that tenants are building up, from year to year, an increasing edifice of debt upon their own shoulders, simply for the purpose of paying their rents, is to assert that which is impossible and incredible. That argument, in fact, cannot be honoured by any serious attention. Of attachment to land, of desire to acquire the tenancy of land, there is no doubt a great deal in Wales. The feeling of land-hunger undoubtedly exists, but it is for the most part harmless, because it has never had the opportunity of indulging itself. If, for example, Welsh landowners, or any considerable number of them, were so ill-advised as to offer the tenancy of vacant farms at auction, it is probable that for a short period land-hunger would enjoy that full meal which would most certainly cure it in the long run. That is to say, a number of men would offer silly and excessive rents; they would be ruined in the long run; their neighbours would learn a lesson from perceiving the results of their folly, and the farms would be ruined also. But land-hunger has never had half a chance of debauching itself in this way, and it is impossible to say how far it is a sentimental appetite for things unattainable, or whether its sharpness would not disappear so soon as the seductive but costly meal was set before it. The writer, having a very high opinion of the commercial genius of his fellow countrymen, is disposed to think that before a full meal land-hunger would disappear. Certainly the fault of Welshmen, of Cardiganshire men for example, has never seemed to him to consist of excessive offers for attainable things.

The next caution to be given to the student of this question, as distinguished from the mere partisan, is to beware of being misled by the red herring of statistics which has been drawn

across the track by both Mr. Thomas Ellis and Mr. Gladstone.
Both these gentlemen are of opinion that the Income Tax
returns, concerning which there has been tedious argument,
supply sufficient material from which to trace the rise and
fall of rents in England and Wales respectively for the last
hundred years. The majority of the Commission are of the
same opinion. The writer is of the contrary opinion. His
views on the statistical question are of no value; nor need
any importance be attached to those of the majority of the
Commission. They have thought fit to criticise his evidence
on the subject at some length, by which he is honoured, nor
does he resent the slightly supercilious tone of their criticism.
It may be worth while, however, to add that the whole of
that evidence was submitted to, and corrected by, an ex-
Secretary of Inland Revenue, who for something like thirty
years had drafted the reports of the Inland Revenue Commissioners.

But this is the proper place at which to state that this
evidence was offered most reluctantly, in the full belief, still
unshaken, that it was accurate, but in the certain conviction
that it was irrelevant. The case was one in which the writer
was convinced that it was a mistake to descend to the
adversary's level and to meet him on false ground of his own
choosing. Over-persuaded by the strong representations of
earnest landowners, the writer gave his evidence, or to speak
more accurately, placed his argument before the Commission,
but he was careful to warn his audience more than once that
the whole argument was absolutely immaterial. In other
words, if we possessed the rental of Wales and the rental of
England for the past hundred years to a penny; if it were
shown that the rental of Wales had risen far more rapidly
than that of England, and had fallen far more slowly, the
result would be simply sundry figures leading to no political
or economical conclusion.

Mark, firstly, that there would be no guarantee that the

rentals of either country rose from a similar standard, and
every reason to believe that they did not, since Wales was, at
the beginning of the century, sparsely populated, remote from
markets, and very inaccessible. Again, it was suggested to
the Commissioners that at the beginning of the century in
Wales, as in England, a system of the leases for lives prevailed, such leases being granted either for political purposes
or in consideration of a premium or fine. Clearly, where
either of these circumstances existed, official figures could
give no intimation of what the true market rental of land
was. But the Commissioners, relying upon the absence
of allusion to fines and premiums by " historical writers,"
and " on the chronic impecuniosity and want of capital from
which, we know, the Welsh farmers have suffered, more or
less, throughout the century," came to the conclusion that
from the middle of the last century to the middle of this
" the payment of fines by occupying tenants in consideration
of leases had been entirely confined to a few estates [prob-
ably only two] in Glamorganshire, to Church property let on
lease to the occupying tenant directly [which was rarely the
case], and possibly to a few other very exceptional cases, but
that, during the last fifty years or more, the practice of levy-
ing such fines may be said to have ceased to exist."

It must be confessed that the suggestion that fines must
be taken into consideration having been made to the Commission late in the day, it had not seemed necessary to the
writer to lay before the Commission direct evidence of a
common practice which was really a matter of common
knowledge. The idea that the old leases were not given for
some consideration, political or pecuniary, had not seemed
likely to be entertained by any body of reasoning men. Of
course, as every practising lawyer in the country districts
knows, the practice of raising the wind in this way was at
one time neither uncommon nor inconvenient; and the Commissioners might have guessed as much, even if they did

not know it, from the answer given by Lord Dunraven's
agent to the question why, in former times, almost the whole
of the Dunraven estate had been let on leases for lives at a
nominal rental.   The agent did not in this specific case
know the history of the transaction ; he merely referred to
the common knowledge of men concerning a very usual
practice. " It was by way of mortgage, I presume, money
borrowed and a lease granted for lives at a nominal rent."
Figures showing large premiums and nominal rents were put
in incidentally in the case of the Rheola estate.   They might
have been put in a great number of other cases ; for that
matter the writer could have quoted some within his personal experience, but it really seemed hardly necessary to
illustrate or to prove the existence of so absolutely familiar
a practice.

But these are matters of mere arithmetic, having no real
significance.   The question, and the only question, is whether
the conditions of the contract between landlord and tenant
in Wales and Monmouthshire are tolerable or intolerable.
Of those conditions rent is one and not necessarily the most
important, and rent means very different things in different
cases.   One must consider the whole contract ; one must
look whether the tenant or the landlord undertakes the duty
of repairing ; whether the landlord or the tenant has spent
money in new buildings and improvements, and so forth.
And even then it is difficult to arrive at any conclusion of
a significant character.

We would, however, direct attention to a series of facts
which entitle the landowners of South Wales and Monmouthshire to great credit for generosity.   No doubt, as will be
shown later, there are many reasons why the rent of farms
should have risen during the present century and particularly
during the latter part of it.   No landowner is to be blamed
simply because it is found that his rents have risen.   But in
the Appendix will be found a series of valuable tables relating

to the different counties of South Wales and to Monmouth-shire, which are replete with significant information. They show, under the hand of every landowner or agent from whom a reply could be obtained, under five columns (1) the land-owner's name; (2) the name and acreage of his estate; (3) abatements granted by him; (4) reductions granted by him; (5) his observations as to the history of the rental of his estate. Of the returns made, every single one, no matter what its quality might be from the point of view of counsel for landowners, was inserted, and we venture to say, without fear of contradiction, that they amount to a magnificent record of consideration shown for tenants in difficulty and of resistance to temptation to raise rents at times when rents might, quite justifiably and properly, have been raised.

We are not, however, concerned to deny that rents have increased, and increased largely, in South Wales during the century, and for very good reason. Nor can that reason be given better than in extracts made from the evidence and language used by the Commissioners. After dilating on the opening of the mineral valleys of the Taff and the Rhondda and the Vale of Neath, on the great development of railway communications in Monmouthshire, Brecon, and Radnor, they go on to say: " We have seen that in at least a few of the counties the increase in rents was contemporaneous with or subsequent to the construction of railways and the provision of improved means of communication." Precisely, that is a part, and a strong part, of the case for Welsh landowners. Then they go on to quote some observations of Mr. Morgan Richardson and Mr. Harford and to add some observations of their own.

Mr. J. C. Harford, of Falcondale, said, with reference to Cardiganshire, that " rents had, of course, been raised in the last fifty years, as fifty years ago that part of the world had no railways, very few roads, and the county itself was swampy and undrained."

"The principle which these statements contain was not, however, contradicted by any of our witnesses, and it is unnecessary to labour it any further. We shall have occasion later to quote the statement made by Sir Joseph Bailey and another witness, with reference to the effect of railway development on rents in the hundred of Builth in Mid-Wales. At this stage, however, we shall limit ourselves to one further quotation, namely, from the evidence given us by Mr. Morgan Richardson of Cardigan. 'A great deal has been said,' he remarked, 'as regards the rise in the value of land in this country as compared with the rise in the value of land in England, and I am prepared to admit that there has been a rise during the last 100 years, and a considerable rise, but I think that the rise is to be explained by particular causes. One cause in this country is that our land is principally grazing land, and the produce of grazing land has risen during the last 100 years, the produce of corn lands having fallen; that a great deal of land is now cultivated which 100 years ago was not in cultivation at all; that roads have been made into the country and through every part of the country, and have developed land which was practically unenclosed 100 years ago; and a very important factor has been the making of railways in this country. The land 80 or 100 years back was far away from the best markets, so that land near the big towns in England had a very much greater advantage over land in this country than it has in the present day, the railway practically bringing us within a short distance of the best markets. And arising from this is the fact that the produce in this country, the grazing land produce, has very materially risen.'

"We may now briefly indicate the periods within which the chief railways were introduced into counties not already mentioned. The South Wales (now the Great Western) Railway reached Carmarthen in September 1852 and Haverfordwest in December 1853, while a branch line from Llanelly

to Llandilo was opened in January 1857 and was shortly
afterwards carried on to Llandovery. The greater portion of
the counties of Carmarthen and Pembroke were thus opened
up in the decade ending in 1862, during which time the
assessed land rental increased 7·7 and 16·1 per cent. respectively. In the former county the main line of railway travels
largely along the seaboard, but in Pembrokeshire it goes
through the heart of the agricultural area, a fact which may
account for the high percentage of the increase within it.
Further branch railways were constructed in both counties in
the following decade, namely, the Pembroke and Tenby line,
opened in 1863, in Pembrokeshire, and two lines from Carmarthen to Pencader and to Llandilo respectively, which
were severally opened in 1864 and 1865, the latter running
through the fertile land of the Vale of Towy. In this decade
a further increase of about 9 per cent. occurred in the rents
of both the counties in question. In this decade also, the
first great rise in the Cardiganshire assessments is to be
noticed (amounting to 17·6 per cent.), a result which must
have been largely due to improved communication : the railway from Carmarthen to Pencader (which is on the border of
Cardiganshire) has been already mentioned as opened in 1864,
and the so-called Manchester and Milford line, which extends
nearly the whole length of Cardiganshire, from Pencader to
Aberystwyth, was made and opened very shortly afterwards,
and about the same time also the Cambrian line was carried
on from Montgomeryshire to Aberystwyth, completing practically all the railway mileage which Cardiganshire possessed
until quite recently.

"As to the county of Montgomery, the first railway opened
within it was that between Newtown and Llanidloes in
August 1859, and its connection, both with Oswestry on the
one side and with Machynlleth on the other, was completed in
1862. The decade from 1852–3 to 1862–3 shows an increase
of 16·4 per cent. in the assessments on land in this country."

Here the Commissioners are on right ground, but they fail to elaborate the case sufficiently. It would surely have been right to remind the public of the growth not only of railways but of population, to speak of the colossal growth of the population of Cardiff, and the grand market offered by it to all the produce of the country. Swansea, Neath, Llanelly, Aberdare, Pontypridd, Newport, and a score of places besides are continually growing. Fresh markets are offered every day, and there is every sign that yet more new markets will be opened continually for many years to come.

Finally the Commissioners arrive at the discovery, not in the least amazing to others, that the rise and fall of rents in the eastern counties of Wales approximates to the rise and fall in the western counties of England, whereas in the western counties of Wales the rise is rather greater and the fall rather less. This is precisely what was to be expected. Western Wales, producing goods which have suffered less in the market than the produce of the rich corn lands, has but recently been opened to the world. It was remote, inaccessible, isolated. Are the Commissioners to be heard to say, as Mr. Gladstone suggested that Welsh landowners were less generous than their brethren of England, that the landowners of the western districts of Wales are harder of heart than those of the eastern? Of saying, or even hinting that, we hesitate to suspect them. No; the rise of rent is the result of the operation of economic forces, which rich landowners may temper and delay; the fall of rent is due to causes over which neither landlord, nor tenant, nor Parliament itself, can exercise the slightest control.

The alleged "approximation" between the eastern counties of Wales and the western counties of England is particularly gratifying to us. As Mr. Knox, Major Birch, and other experts have testified that the Welsh tenant is certainly under no disadvantage as compared with his English brother when his farm is valued for purposes of rental, so the Commissioners have ascertained that where England and Wales border upon one another, where conditions of farming are approximately the same, rents also approximate in their fluctuation. It follows, as of necessity, that the Welsh landowner is of like flesh and blood with his fellow landowner in England, actuated by like principles, moved by like motives, a partner in the same humanity. Now, the Welsh landowner asks for no better treatment than is to be accorded to the English; and never has asked for any special favour. His case, therefore, is virtually won, his protest against special legislation for Wales undeniably succeeds by virtue of the facts collected and the figures analysed by the Commissioners.

CHAPTER VI

ENOUGH has been written and demonstrated to convince all save the most prejudiced minds that the circumstances which were, in our judgment, unwisely held to justify the establishment of judicial rents in Ireland, simply do not exist in South Wales or in Monmouthshire, and it is deemed unnecessary to repeat here, from another volume which has for some time been at the disposal of members of both Houses, the economical and other arguments which condemn the establishment of any such system. The result of them may, however, be summarised thus : A system of judicial rents is essentially reactionary, since it is founded upon the entirely exploded principle which underlay the Statute of Labourers and, as Irish experience shows, the attempt to establish such a system results in evils at least as great as those which judicial rents were invented to remedy. But, since the evils themselves do not exist in Wales, it has been deemed prudent to demonstrate that fact by way of shutting the door finally against the Land Courts which the majority of the Commission propose to establish, in which proposal they are supported by the Welsh Radical members of Parliament.

We now approach the consideration of two subjects very closely connected with one another at bottom, albeit the connection may not, at first sight, appear manifest. They are Fixity of Tenure and Compensation for Improvements made by the tenant ; and the position to be adopted generally upon these two questions is that, assuming sufficient provision to be made for compensation for improvements, no substantial reason can be found for conferring fixity of tenure upon the sitting tenant, while many reasons may be urged against endowing him with this kind of property. This may, at the first blush, seem a hard saying; but it will appear in another light when it is explained; and it may be permissible to state that it comes from a man who understands and shares the Celtic habit of "clinging to the old home." Only, it must be understood sentiment and sympathy have their own particular domain and law has its separate province. Law can compel a man, landlord or tenant, to be just in his dealings; but it may be predicted with safety that, if once law attempts to adopt a sentimental attitude, or to compel men to show substantial sympathy on other than commercial grounds, the results will certainly be absurd and dangerous.

It is plain from the mass of the evidence in the whole of the Principality and in Monmouthshire that never was the claim for fixity of tenure, standing alone, made with less justification than in Wales.

Succession in tenancy is practically hereditary. The rule was well stated by Colonel Hughes, the Wynnstay agent. "The custom of continuous family succession in tenancy has always been a predominant feature on this estate; in fact, on the Welsh portion it is and has been the invariable rule to accept a member of the deceased tenant's family as his successor." This practice, as Colonel Hughes goes on to say, is followed even in the case of widows. What say the Commission? "The same practice of hereditary succession prevails on most other large estates throughout Wales, the most notable examples being found, perhaps, on the properties of the Earl of Powis, Lord Penhryn, and Mr. Assheton Smith, though similar examples are not lacking, as we shall presently see, in South Wales. *There is certainly a much larger number of tenants who can boast of an uninterrupted family connection*

F

with the same holdings extending over several centuries than there is of estate owners or of occupying freeholders whose families have succeeded each other in the ownership of their respective properties for an equal period."

Evidence similar to that of North Wales was given in less detail, and never challenged, in regard to the estates of Lord Cawdor, Sir James Hills Johnes, V.C., Colonel Turberville (who deposed to the practice in the Vale of Glamorgan, as did two Pembrokeshire farmers to that of Pembrokeshire), Lord Lisburne, Mr. J. C. Harford (Lampeter), Captain Jones Parry (Newcastle Emlyn). Sir Joseph Bailey and Mr. Williams Vaughan deposed to the practice in the county of Brecon. Hundreds of other cases might have been quoted. But after a time it became clear that there was no use in labouring a point which was admitted, or in adducing multitudinous instances to prove a custom having its origin in friendly feeling and not in law, the prevalence of which was common ground.

The evidence as to changes of tenancy bears on this point, and the Commission writes strangely on the matter. "Unfortunately," begins the draughtsman, "we have no means of ascertaining whether changes of tenancy are, on the whole, now more frequent than they were at the commencement of the century." But all the evidence laid before the Commission tended to show that changes were rare, and they summarised it, referring to the evidence of Lord Cawdor's agent ("In the thirty years of my management we have had an average of one change a year") and to that of Mr. Davies, of Froodvale, who is agent for many estates. Then they take an accusation of numerous charges made in relation to the Lawrenny estate, of which Mr. Stokes, the agent, was able to dispose by showing that in all cases save one, since 1875, the initiative had come from the tenants. Then they commit themselves to the opinion that "in many parts of the country, especially on the smaller and more scattered estates, changes of tenancy are greatly on the increase." This very general statement, however, is supported almost exclusively by general statements on the part of witnesses, and, on a matter of this kind, general statements carry little or no weight. Nor is the mere mention of specific farms on which there have been many changes significant. Changes may be made at the wish of tenants; for excellent reasons by landowners; each case must be examined thoroughly before it can be decided whether, if the landlord compelled the tenant to remove, his reasons were adequate, or, if the tenant left by his own wish, it was because the conditions of his tenure were insupportable. It may be said with justice that the Commission had neither time nor opportunity to investigate thoroughly each instance alleged; and if any accusation were made against the Commission on this head, this excuse, saving for the days wasted on immaterialities, would be good. But the question is not whether the Commission acted properly, but whether certain classes of evidence upon which the Commission appears to rely are entitled to carry weight. Unsifted evidence cannot be improved in quality by the fact that it could not be sifted. An unwinnowed mixture of grain and chaff remains unwinnowed, whatever reason there may have been for not winnowing it.

Looking through the whole of the evidence, it is clear that the Commission, holding that "it is only natural to assume that, in common with all classes, the agricultural population were more stationary prior to the great industrial development which has been so marked a characteristic of the last hundred years," have not been able to establish any remarkable increase in changes of tenancy. In other words, tenancy is reasonably secure in Wales.

But it may be said—indeed, it was frequently urged by tenants and others before the Commission—that, although changes are not frequent, and although in practice tenancy is reasonably secure in Wales, tenants hesitate to make perma-

nent improvements because, apart from the compensation
secured to them by the Agricultural Holdings Act of 1883,
the improvements once made, they are at the mercy of their
landlords.   If the law were otherwise, they say, many
improvements would be made and the productive powers of
the land would be much increased.   There is perhaps some
room for doubt as to the accuracy of this view.   There is
hardly a large estate upon which it is not the custom for the
landlord to provide, at his own cost, every reasonable improvement which is likely to pay, without charging any
additional rent.   The tenant, it is true, has to do the
haulage, but that is all.   The prudent tenant will probably
always prefer to avail himself of this custom as long as it
endures.

    But there is something to be said for the tenant's point of
view.   It can but rarely happen that a landlord, succeeding
to a dilapidated estate, can afford to put the whole of it in
order at once.   It must often happen that the tenant is better
equipped with capital, in proportion to his requirements,
than the landlord.   It is clearly right that he should be in a
position to improve securely, that is to say, in the certainty
that the law will not permit him to be deprived of the
improved value of his holding, either by eviction or by
rent raised upon his improvement.   Rare as such cases may
be, it is not to be denied that there are embarrassed landowners, in Wales as in England, and that hardships may
occur, and sometimes do occur, under the present law.   It is
not pretended that Welsh landowners, or any others, are
archangels.   They have made out, undoubtedly, a strong case
for themselves; they have given, as a body, a good account of
their stewardship.   But the body of landlords, as of tenants,
contains individuals of every degree of intelligence, high and
low; of every variety of character, good and bad.   It is no
more right that the improving tenant should be at the mercy
of his landlord in some measure, or should be deterred from

improving by the feeling of insecurity, than that the landlord should be, as the majority of the Commission seem to wish, at the mercy of the tenant.

But, it is submitted with some confidence, if some other efficient remedy for a state of things which ought not to exist can be suggested, then statutory fixity of tenure is the very last remedy to be applied; and the reasons are not far to seek. Firstly, statutory fixity of tenure involves, as of absolute necessity, sundry other institutions by way of corollary. Take, for example, the Land Bill of Mr. Bryn Roberts, M.P., which provides that a tenant shall not be compulsorily ejected save for certain specified causes, amongst them being failure to pay his rent. It follows that, as an aid to statutory fixity of tenure, the settlement of rent by some external authority must be provided for. To illustrate this the writer may be permitted to recount a case within his own professional experience. He was asked to advise a large hotelkeeper in London desirous of getting rid of a guest who, having taken one of the cheapest rooms in the hotel, took neither meat nor drink therein and was unprofitable. It seemed to him doubtful (that doubt was dispelled after an expensive law-suit quite recently) whether the innkeeper had a legal right simply to turn the guest out. He therefore advised that the charge for room No. 126 should be revised, should, in fact, be doubled from day to day. So without any lawsuit at all the guest quitted. That is what an unwelcome tenant might have to do if there were fixity of tenure without a Land Court. Therefore if you establish fixity of tenure, you must establish a Land Court also; and the objections to a Land Court are well known.

But the worst objection to statutory fixity of tenure is that it is an unnecessary invasion of the landlord's rights, tending to diminish the value of his property and of all landed property, including that of the smallest freeholder, and at the same time to produce a state of things on occasion which is distinctly not to be encouraged, and emphatically not to the public interest. Let us take a case from North Wales for example as recorded in the evidence. There a tenant declared that he had been turned out of his farm for political reasons; his agent, on the contrary, averred that the true reason was persistent poaching on the part of the tenant, and in this case, as a conviction of the tenant for poaching was proved, one may be permitted not only to believe the agent, but to say that no reasoning being can disbelieve him. Now it is not necessary to express an opinion on the question whether poaching is a sufficient excuse for getting rid of a tenant, but it is certain that there are many good reasons conceivable for getting rid of a tenant which are not likely to be scheduled in any Act of Parliament, and which, many of them, would be remarkably difficult to prove in a Court of Law. A man may be sulky and insolent whenever he meets his landlord, he may make his farm an eyesore, he may do many unpleasant things which make him undesirable as a neighbour. The natural sequel is a state of permanent hostility between landlord and tenant, which is not good for either of them or for the land.

As matters stand, evictions of any kind are admittedly very rare, but the fact that a landlord can, as a last resource, rid himself of a disagreeable neighbour if he is so disposed, undoubtedly lends part of its value to landed estate, which, regarded as a mere pecuniary investment, is the worst in the world. No wise man will give as much for land planted with tenants whom he cannot remove as he will for land subject only to the conditions which now prevail. If, therefore, there is no necessity for so impairing the value of land, it seems a pity to introduce statutory fixity of tenure.

Now, to take a common-sense view of the matter, what are the real rights, moral, not merely legal, of the tenant? Leaving sentiment, usually a very expensive luxury, on one side, they are that he shall not be turned out of his holding without receiving full compensation for improvements. Full compensation for improvements is the root of the whole matter. It was admitted by several intelligent witnesses, who came forward to support proposals for agrarian legislation of the most revolutionary character, that full compensation for improvements would remove every grievance. Now, full compensation, even generous compensation, is, in the writer's experience (which in this matter may, without immodesty, be called unique) an idea which is welcomed with open arms by almost every landowner and agent in Wales. In other words, no man desires to confiscate the fruits of his tenant's labour and expense, and at the same time, no man, except here and there a politician with electioneering ends to serve, will consent without a struggle to be deprived of his freedom in dealing with his property.

And here we come to a curious phenomenon, which is well worthy of the attention of members of Parliament. The Agricultural Holdings Act of 1893 is, as everybody knows, an absolute and peremptory statute. No man, landlord or tenant, can contract himself out of it effectually; it is supposed to govern them, will they or no. Yet, over the greater part of the county of Glamorgan, which, besides containing half the population of Wales and the best markets, is remarkably well farmed, this Act is confessedly a dead letter. Nobody attempts to contract out of it; for the plain fact is that nobody takes the slightest notice of it. This is simply because, in the opinion of landlords and tenants alike, the customs of East and West Glamorganshire respectively are infinitely more suitable to the requirements of the country, and far more adequate in every way than the Agricultural Holdings Act of 1883. These customs, the growth of which does great credit to both parties to the contract of tenancy, are, very properly, treated at some length in the Report. They have reached their present state by many successive steps, some of them, no doubt, accompanied by some tribulation; it is not even suggested here that they are perfect. But it is a noteworthy fact that, when Parliament produced the Act of 1883 as a kind of Farmers' Charter, the agricultural interest in Glamorganshire were so far advanced on the way to fair dealing between landlord and tenant that they were able with one accord to cast the Farmers' Charter on one side.

Meanwhile, over the rest of Wales, and over the whole of England also, the Agricultural Holdings Act of 1883 is the governing law. True it is that it was asserted that landlords sometimes purported to contract themselves out of it, but in the vast majority of cases, when specific instances were quoted, the charge broke down hopelessly. Either it was found that the Act avoided was that of 1875, which was avoidable, or that the witness had misconstrued the alleged contract. Sometimes, too, the document produced was an undated and alleged copy, an absurd thing to produce under any circumstances. True it is also that, on a great many large estates, a better and more generous scale of compensation was, as the Act permits, very properly substituted for the statutory scale. But there are large estates and small, and, as there has been occasion to observe before, it is unreasonable to demand that small properties shall be managed by experts of the same class as the agents of large estates.

What is the main purpose of this statute? It is to regulate the relations between landlord and tenant when the time comes for their parting company, and that time may come at the option of either party. The tenant may give notice of his intention to quit. When he quits, the Act purports to regulate the payments, if any, to be made to the tenant, the manner in which the amount to be paid shall be assessed, and so forth. It is submitted that the landowner is in all cases well within his rights, moral as well as legal, in standing by the letter of the Act. For the Act says in effect, " You are neither of you to be trusted to make your own bargains. The law shall settle the matter for you." In the face of that it cannot reasonably be said that the landowner is under any moral obligation to depart from the statute.

As a matter of fact, the statute is, by universal admission, grossly defective and unfair to tenant and landowner both in England and Wales. Its machinery is cumbrous and expensive, it abounds in technicalities and pitfalls for the unwary, its scales of compensation are unelastic and frequently inapplicable, it is grossly unjust to the landowner in at least one important respect, and it has never done much good to any class of men save those of the profession to which the writer has the honour to belong. But every evil in it which is felt in Wales is felt more keenly in England, where changes are, unfortunately, far more numerous, and it is understood— the matter indeed was mentioned in the Queen's Speech—that her Majesty's Government have every intention of introducing a comprehensive measure dealing with the grievances not only of the tenant, but also of the landowner, not merely of the Principality, but of England also. In relation to that Bill Mr. Walter Long will undoubtedly have the cordial support of all Welsh landowners.

CHAPTER VII

IN this chapter three points remain to be dealt with. It will be remembered that Mr. Morgan Richardson, than whom none has a better right to speak, gave some powerful and touching evidence at Cardigan concerning the condition of the mortgaged freeholders, and described the hardships, the misery, and the utter hopelessness of their struggle for life. Mr. Morgan Richardson, be it observed, is a member of the Executive Committee of this Association, and the sympathetic tone of his evidence may go some way to convince our accusers that this society, falsely described in the Report as a political organisation, is not wanting in sympathy for the distress, varying in different districts and at different times, under which the Welsh peasantry undoubtedly suffer. So deeply were the Commission impressed by the earnestness and the thoughtfulness of Mr. Morgan Richardson's statement that, at their request, he attended before them again and entered into his scheme in greater detail.

That scheme may be summarised in a very few lines. The freeholders of Cardiganshire are on the brink of ruin, especially those who have purchased within the last twenty or thirty years; in fact, unless relief comes, they are ruined. But the State might advance the money necessary to pay off the mortgages with safety, for the market price of the land is high, the security is good, and the freeholders might certainly be relied upon to pay such a yearly sum as would give the

State fair interest on its money and make a yearly instalment of the principal.

It was plain from the outset that all depended upon the security. If the security was, as Mr. Morgan Richardson said, safe and good, the State might wisely advance the money, and so save the freeholders. There is probably not a man or woman in Wales who would not hail with delight the salvation of a class which has produced quite an extraordinary number of the most prominent personages in Wales. But this is a hard and businesslike world. If circumstances arose to impair the value of the security it was plain that the State could not, in fairness to other citizens, advance the money, and that the freeholders must perish, as now they certainly will.

Now, Mr. Morgan Richardson expressed his decided opinion that the establishment of a system of judicial rents would so impair the market value of land that, assuming that system to be established, the security would become insufficient.

As is well known, Parliament, early in the present session, was asked to sanction the advance of money to freeholders thus cruelly embarrassed, but Parliament refused its assent. Why? Surely for the plainest of reasons. The Report of the Commission had been issued, it had painted the condition of Wales in lurid colours, it had described a terror-stricken peasantry, and the majority had recommended the establishment of a Land Court. As the land agitation and the proceedings of the Commission had caused sundry mortgagees of Welsh land to call in their money, and others who had money to lend to refuse Welsh land as a security, so this wild recommendation of a Land Court destroyed the last lingering hope of the Welsh peasant-freeholders. For that recommendation they have to thank Earl Carrington, Mr. Brynmor Jones, Q.C., M.P., Mr. Richard Jones, Mr. Griffiths, Mr. Grove and Principal Rhys.

For the rest the writer desires to make a personal explanation. He had the honour of conducting the case for landowners, or of taking part in its conduct (so far as the methods of the Commission permitted) in Wales and Monmouthshire. Very early in the proceedings, at Carnarvon in the first place, an endeavour was made to introduce a question of title. The witness in the box was Colonel the Honourable W. E. Sackville West; the question asked affected the title of Lord Penrhyn's property. The writer had deemed it prudent to advise Colonel West, and others also, to decline to answer any questions going to title, and his advice was followed. The same principle was pursued throughout the proceedings; and would be pursued again, in the event of the recurrence of any similar proceedings. It has been suggested since that Lord Penrhyn was afraid of showing his title, but that is sheer nonsense. This question of title was sprung on Colonel West without a moment's notice; it was impossible that he should answer it, for he had not the necessary knowledge. Every lawyer will perceive and know that the examination of a title is a tedious, delicate, and expensive business, not to be undertaken save for some very substantial reason. Men do not fling their titles in the air for every daw to peck at, and the writer gave his advice deliberately, in the belief that if the Crown had intended to promote an investigation of titles, a Commission of very different constitution and powers would have been appointed, and the intention would have been very plainly stated. Neither owner, nor agent, nor lawyer, carries the title of a historic estate in his pocket to show to any passer-by. In fact, the contention of the Commission was irrational. The case of Colonel West is used for illustration, as showing the thoughtless and haphazard way in which Commissioners asked questions which, whatever may have been the object with which they were asked, distinctly went to the question of title.

A more audacious and irrelevant effort was made in South

Wales, where a long attack was made upon the Duke of Beaufort in relation to the rights in the foreshore at Swansea. This, to be entertained by an agricultural Commission, was a marvellous topic, but it was one into which the writer did not feel disposed to enter. Firstly, it was deliriously irrelevant; secondly, a long and expensive suit involving the whole question of title had been decided in the Duke's favour by the Court of Exchequer some fifty years ago, and the opinion of that court seemed preferable to that of the Commission. Thirdly, the main argument of the worthy witnesses from the Swansea Corporation seemed to be that it would be much more convenient to Swansea if they were empowered to take the Duke's property without payment. That proposition, since it was self-evident, it seemed hardly necessary to controvert.

Then the Commission complain of the Board of Trade on the following ground. It appears that prior to 1888 the Crown and the Marquis of Bute were at issue as to the ownership of a portion of the foreshore at Cardiff. "The local advisers of the Board (we understand the advisers at Cardiff) thought the Marquis of Bute had a strong case, but nothing was laid before us to show how far they were in a position to give sound advice upon so difficult a matter of law and fact." So say the Commissioners. The Board of Trade yielded the claim made by Lord Bute in consideration of £6055. Of this the Commissioners complain, on the ground of public policy, and observe "No one on behalf of the Marquis of Bute explained his title." The writer is of opinion that he ought to have been disbarred for sheer lunacy if he had permitted any explanation to be made when one title, at any rate, was absolutely proved, and the matter was entirely outside the competence of the Commission.

For the rest, apart from the question of squatters, which is really too trivial to enter upon, all the principal points raised by the Commission have been treated. They complain, from time to time, of sales of Crown lands; those sales are irrevocable, and if some bargains have turned out well, others have turned out badly. They complain of enclosures of waste land made under Act of Parliament; it is waste of ink and lamentation. Their business was to inquire into the conditions of agricultural life in Wales; their excursions by the way do not concern us. It is enough to have shown, almost out of their mouths, that the cases of Wales and England are identical in character, and that in degree Wales is the more fortunate; and finally that there is no substance in the cry for special legislation for Wales.

APPENDIX.

The following are the figures and statements as to abatements, reductions, and history of rental under the hands of the landowners and agents making the returns. None have been omitted.

RADNORSHIRE.

Name and Address of Landowner	Estate	Abatements	Reductions	Observations as to the History of Rents
Mrs. E. R. Banks and W. H. Banks Ridgebourne, Kington	(In Radnor and Brecon 1875 acres)	10 p.c. has been returned to tenant on several farms. On a few a year's or half-year's rent has been written off	Since 1877 some rents have been reduced 25 p.c., others less	The estate as a whole has not been re-valued, but most of the rents have been reduced. No rents have been raised except for additional buildings, upon which the tenant pays a percentage
Mrs. S. J. Bryan	Crunogoel (1080 acres)	We have on many occasions given something back, but cannot say what percentage. All has depended on the need of the case	Since 1877 the rents have been permanently reduced 15 to 20 p.c.	—

RADNORSHIRE—*(continued)*.

Name and Address of Landowner	Estate	Abatements	Reductions	Observations as to the History of Rents
J. P. Chesment Severn	Penybont Hall. (In Radnor and Montgomery, 10,900 acres)	10 p.c. abatement has been granted in the years 1886, 1887, 1888, and 1892	Since 1877 rents have been permanently reduced in five cases—average 12 p.c.	The estate has not been revalued within the last 100 years. During the last half century practically no rents have been raised; interest has been charged for draining and fencing under enclosure awards, which the landlord has got to keep in good repair
John Corrie Carter Cefnfaes, Rhayader	Upper Cefnfaes (39 acres)	I have made no abatements, except where I have by arrangement taken small portions into my own hands from the tenant for plantations, &c.	—	—
Mrs. Gibson-Watt Doldowlod, Rhayader	Doldowlod, Rock House, Boatside, and New Radnor. (In Radnor and Brecon, 9500 acres)	An abatement of 10 to 15 p.c. was made from 1880 to 1885; 15 to 20 p.c. from 1886 to 1889 according to age of tenancies; 5 to 10 p.c. from 1889 to 1891	In 1892 all farms were let title free and a permanent reduction of 5 to 10 p.c., made and a further temporary abatement of 10 p.c. allowed, which, we have reason to believe, according to age of tenancies, satisfied all the tenants	The estate has not been revalued within the last 50 years. During that period rents have been raised in a few cases where change of tenancy has taken place, but in each case the farms now let at 5 p.c. below the valuation made

George Augustus Haig, Pen Ithon	Pen Ithon. (From 2400 to 2500 acres)	I have frequently made abatements of 10 and 20 p.c., and during the last three years have given maize—usually one sack of maize for about £10 of rental. But there is a farm on my property at the rent it brought in up to 1879. Besides this I now give lime free and do a great deal of fencing, while before 1879 the tenants all kept up their own fencing, buying wood out of their own pockets	There is not a farm on my property that has not been reduced 20 p.c. and many farms very much more. Pen Cwm was once let at £550, then at £450, now at £250; Dulley Bank used to let at £225; it is now let in two divisions for £130 (£90 and £40); Gorse used to let at £40, now for £28; Lower Llaithddu used to let at £56, now at £40 with 6 acres moreland. The farms, owing to the growth of the plantations, ought to have improved in rent as shelter is valuable, and had prices of stock and other things remained the same they would have improved	Undoubtedly my rents have been raised. They were £454 and £30 when I bought, but for each £1 spent in purchase money I have spent £3 in permanent improvements—planting, enclosing, draining, road-making, new and greatly extended farm-buildings of all sorts. I was spending my own money and therefore reckoned no interest on the money I spent. Had I been spending borrowed money the income would not have paid one-third of the interest
Sir H. E. F. Lewis, Bart. Harpton Court, Kington	Harpton Court (10,000 acres)	From March 25, 1886, to September 29, 1888, also from September 29, 1891, to September 29, 1892, the tenants were allowed 10 p.c. reduction on their rents	Permanent reductions of rent amounting to £610 a year have been made	The estate was valued in 1864, the result being, as far as I know, a slight increase of the rental. During the last half-century, in a few instances, on a change of tenancy, rents were raised, but have been again reduced
P. C. Milbank, Norton, Presteigne	Norton. (3000 acres)	An abatement of 10 p.c. was granted last year and a promise of 15 p.c. for two more	Since 1877 some rents have been permanently reduced	The estate was valued last year when I purchased the property; the result is that it reduces receipts very slightly

RADNORSHIRE—(*continued*).

Name and Address of Landowner	Estate	Abatements	Reductions	Observations as to the History of Rents
Lord Ormathwaite Eywood, Titley	Llandewy, Cefnllys, and Gladestry. (13,500 acres)	10 p.c. abatement was made to all tenants in 1887, 1888, and 1892	The rent-roll since my succeeding has been reduced by £246	The estate, to the best of my belief, has not been re-valued during the last 50 years. I have in no single case raised a rent since I have been in possession. In two instances, where the old tenants gave up farms to take larger ones in Shropshire, I received more from the new tenants than from the old
Mrs. G. H. Philips Abbey Cwm Hir	Abbey Cwm Hir (7750 acres)	Very liberal allowances have been made, varying from 20 to 5 p.c. for many years	No reductions are required, as the estate is very justly rented	The estate has been re-valued, but the valuation was not acted upon. No rents have been raised during the last half-century
Hon. Horace Plunkett, M.P. Mount Street, London	Begwildy (1300 acres)	A percentage has been returned to some of the tenants during last three years	The rent has been reduced about 5 p.c. since 1885	—
Charles Coltman Rogers Stanage Park, Brampton Brian	Stanage Park, Cwmgilla. (3700 acres)	Abatements of 10 p.c. were made on all rents due September 29, 1879; 10 p.c. on rents due September 29, 1885; the latter was continued half-yearly till March 25, 1888, when rents were all reconsidered and some reductions made permanent	Since 1877, nearly all rents have been permanently reduced, amounting to £320 or about 11½ p.c. on the rental	The estate has not been re-valued. No rents have been raised since 1878

Major-General J. R. and Mrs. Sladen, Rhydoldog, Rhayader	Rhydoldog (4823 acres)	5 p.c returned whenever depression of farming interest made it necessary. For the last two years, from 7 to 10 p.c. returned	One small farm has been reduced	The estate was re-valued in 1874 or 1875
W. W. Thomas-Moore, Old Hall, Llanvihangel	Old Hall, Maesgwynne and other small estates. (2960 acres)	10 p.c. of the last half-year's rent	Permanent reduction of rent-roll £245	The estate has not been revalued. Rents have not been raised within the last 20 years

BRECONSHIRE.

Earl of Ashburnham, Dover Street, W.	Talgarth (2533 acres)	15 p.c. in 1877 and 1888; 5 p.c. on one half-year in 1889; and 15 p.c. on one half-year in 1892	One farm rented in 1873 at £600 was reduced to £500 in 1877; another rented in 1882 at £90 was reduced in 1886 to £70	No rents have been raised except when land adjoining the town of Talgarth has come on hand by the death of tenants, and has been let in plots for accommodation purposes
Marquis Camden	Brecknockshire estates. (7500 acres)	10 p.c. in 1880 and 1891, 1895-8 and 1892, 15 p.c. in 1893	Rent of four farms reduced from total of £654 to £555	Estate was re-valued in 1856, and some of the rents were then raised as found necessary. Since then the rents have been adjusted from time to time on changes of tenancy and the nominal rental is now about 7½ p.c. above that of 1856, before the valuation then made

BRECONSHIRE—(continued).

Name and Address of Landowner	Estate	Abatements	Reductions	Observations as to the History of Rents
Mrs. E. R. Banks and W. H. Banks, Ridgebourne, Kington	(In Radnor and Brecon, 1875 acres)	10 p.c. has been returned to tenant on several farms. On a few, a year's, or half-year's, rent has been written off	Since 1877 some rents have been reduced 25 p.c.; others less	The estate as a whole has not been re-valued, but most of the rents have been reduced. No rents have been raised except for additional buildings, upon which the tenant pays a percentage
Mrs. Bold. Boughrood Castle	Llanfilhangel (830 acres)	—	One farm to 1884 was let at £220, is now £180. Another farm and by tach till 1880 was let at £320; for the farm I have £180, for the by tach the agreement is £60, but I have never received so much	—
J. D. Dickinson, Ystradarallt, Nantgaredig	Glanhonddu (1000 acres)	I have not, since 1877, granted any abatements	I have reduced one farm from £210 to £180, and another farm from £150 to £130	
Mrs. E. H. Gibson-Watt, Doldowlod, Rhayader	Doldowlod, Rock House, New Radnor. (In Radnor and Brecon, 9500 acres)	An abatement of 10 to 15 p.c. was made from 1880 to 1885; 15 to 20 p.c. from 1886 to 1889, according to age of tenancies; 5 to 10 p.c. from 1890 to 1891	In 1892 all the farms were let tithe free, and a permanent reduction of 5 to 10 p.c. made, and a further temporary abatement of 10 p.c. allowed, which we have reason to believe, according to the age of tenancies, satisfied all the tenants	Rents have been raised in a few cases where a change of tenancy has taken place, but in each case the farms were let at 5 p.c. below the valuation made

E. H. Greenly · Titley Court	Oakfield, Caeran (2000 acres)	1879, 1880, 15 and 10 p.c.; 1881, 1882, 1883, 1884, some 10 p.c.; 1885, some 15 p.c.; 1887, 1888, some 10 p.c.; 1892, 10 p.c.	1881, permanent reduction in most cases of 15 p.c.; 1885, permanent reduction in most cases of 15 p.c. The total reduction of rent roll since 1877 has been something over 20 p.c.	So far as I know the rents have not been raised during the last 50 years. The property has been in my possession about 20 years
Mrs. Gwyn · Dyffryn, Neath	Abererare (2145 acres)	Abatements are frequently granted. Amounts of 10 p.c., 15 p.c., and 20 p.c. have been remitted to individual tenants —lease-holders as well as yearly tenants. 10 p.c. all round was remitted at the last rent audit	Many of the rents have been permanently reduced. During the last 12 years ending September 29, 1892, the rental of the Breconshire estate has been reduced about 10 p.c. all round	—
Capt. Howell Jones-Williams · Cui Park, Talybont	Coity Mawr and Cui (2000 acres)	On many occasions I have granted abatements of rent	Roughly, I have reduced seven farms £175	—
James Lewis · Aberdare	Glyncollwng (In Brecon and Glamorgan, 1800 acres)	10 p.c. for the last seven years, excepting in 1889–90; and 15 p.c. for the last half-year ending August 1892	No permanent reductions	—

APPENDIX.

BRECONSHIRE—(*continued*)

Name and Address of Landowner	Estate	Abatements	Reductions	Observations as to the History of Rents
Sir W. T. Lewis, Bart. Aberdare	Cwmtâf. (In Brecon, Glamorgan, Carmarthen, and Monmouth, 1200 acres)	An abatement of 10 p.c. per annum has been granted to the Cwmtâf tenants for the half-years ending Michaelmas 1891, Lady Day 1892, and Michaelmas 1892, respectively. Two of these farms, purchased in 1888, were then subject to an abatement of 10 p.c., which abatement has been continued, in addition to the further abatement of 10 p.c. in 1891 and 1892. Another farm in Breconshire has been reduced from £40 to £30 per annum for the last six years	—	I have only acquired the farms within the last 20 years, and there has been no re-valuation since they have come into my possession, nor have the rents been raised
Capt. Lloyd-Harries . Llandilo	(In Brecon and Carmarthen, 5811 acres)	10 p.c. allowed at Michaelmas 1885, Lady Day and Michaelmas 1886 and 1887, Lady Day 1888, and Lady Day and Michaelmas 1892	In some cases reductions have been made	The estate was re-valued in 1877, the result being a small increase in some places not amounting to 3 p.c. on the rental
T. Lloyd-Barrow (for his wife, the owner of two-thirds of the Lloyd estate)	Lloyd. (In Brecon and Carmarthen, 4457 acres)	20 p.c. in November last, and 10 p.c. for the audit now due promised	—	—

R. H. Mausel, as trustee for Mrs. Mausel and own property	(In Monmouth, Glamorgan, and Brecon, 500 acres)	Since 1877 the following abatements have been given : 5 p.c. 6¾ p.c., 17 p.c., 9 p.c., 10 p.c., and 8 p.c.				The last time the estate was re-valued was in 1837, during my father's life. A few farms becoming vacant were re-valued some years ago with an increase of rental since reduced
Hugh P. Powel. Castle Madoc, Brecon	Castle Madoc (2750 acres)	I have since 1877 given back 10 p.c. on several occasions		Most of my farms have been permanently reduced, excepting those where rents have not been raised for nearly half a century or those which are let as accommodation land		
Rev. David Price, 18 Castle Street, Brecon	Noyadd Farm and Brintymawr. (199 acres)	I have allowed a rebate for several years on Noyadd of 25 p.c., and last year I have reduced the rent to that extent		On Noyadd farm, one-fourth. On Brintymawr I have made no reduction, as the farm is let at a very low rental		Although I have had two or three tenants on each farm, the rent has not been increased since I came into possession some 30 years ago
Trustees of the late Miss Charlotte Story-Maskelyne	Losgoed (3300 acres)	From September 1879 till September 1885 a 10 p.c. abatement (in some instances more) was regularly made. In one or two instances, in lieu of the 10 p.c., more than an equivalent was allowed in the form of a remission of a portion of local rates or other allowance. During this period on one holding, in lieu of 10 p.c., there was allowed, in March 1880, 15 p.c.; in September 1881, 20 p.c.; in March 1882, 23 p.c.; in September 1882, 27 p.c.; in March 1883, 37 p.c.; in September 1883, 30 p.c.; in September 1884, 26 p.c.; and in March 1885 this holding was permanently reduced 33 p.c.		In 1885 and 1886 a permanent reduction was made amounting to 26 p.c. on the old rent-roll, and the rents have since remained at the same figure, except that one holding was increased 14¾ p.c. from March 1890 till September 1892, when the 14¾ p.c. was taken off again		The estate has not been valued for purposes of rental so far as the owners are aware during the last 50 years. No rents have been raised in the last 20 years except as noted in the previous column, and this was under a mutual arrangement between landlord and tenant in view of the heavy reduction previously made

BRECONSHIRE—(continued).

Name and Address of Landowner	Estate	Abatements	Reductions	Observations as to the History of Rents
Miss Clara Thomas, Llwynmadoc	Llwynmadoc (9728 acres)	Abatements for three half-years ending Michaelmas 1886, of 15 p.c.; and for two half-years, ending Michaelmas 1892, of 10 p.c.	Taking the rental of 1853 as the basis; the rental in 1863 was 2 p.c. higher: in 1878, 23·9 p.c. higher: and in 1893 is 4·8 p.c. higher than the rental in 1853. The general rise, based on a new valuation, took place in 1874, amounting on the whole to 22 p.c. The general reduction amounting to 14 p.c. took effect from Michaelmas 1886. Individual reductions made at various times since 1876 account for the further 5 p.c. of reduction	The estate was valued by J. M. Davies, of Frondyale, Lalndilo, in 1873. His valuation was 26·2 higher than the rental in 1855. The rents were raised as the result of this valuation 22 p.c. on the 1855 rental
A. V. H. Vaughan-Lee, Dillington Park, Ilminster	Lanllay. (In Glamorgan and Brecon, 5800 acres)	No general reduction or abatement has been made, but in some instances allowances have been made	Taking the whole of the farm rental it is 7 p.c. less now than in 1877	No general re-valuation has taken place, but in some instances rents have been altered. Comparing the rental of a portion of the property (about 3500 acres), the difference in the rental between the present time and 50 years ago is £14 10s. in favour of the present time

J. E. Vaughan. Rheola, Neath	Rheola. (In Glamorgan and Brecon, 5800 acres)	On occasions abatements have been made in individual cases; but no general abatement has been made, the rents having remained unaltered for a very long period.	The rent-roll from farms on this estate is about 4 p.c. lower than it was in 1887, and in some cases the lands are let tithe free, which increases the percentage of reduction by about another 2 p.c., making in all 6 p.c. reduction	There has been no general valuation of the property during the last 50 years. A considerable portion of it had been let at nominal rents for lives by a former owner, a fine having been taken, and as these fell in the farms were re-let at fair rents
Miss Susan Williams Trephilip	Pentrezwyn (200 acres)	I gave back 10 p.c. per annum in 1879, the times being so bad, and this continued till 1885, when I permanently lowered the rent	I permanently reduced the rent £30 in 1885, viz., from £120 to £90	—
Lieut.-Col. Wood Gwernyfed Park, Three Cocks	Gwernyfed (5227 acres)	Percentage returned:— 10 per cent. in 1885 15 ,, 1886 15 ,, 1887 10 ,, 1888 2½ ,, 1889 10 ,, 1891 12½ ,, 1892 20 p.c. on losses of sheep by liver rot in 1880	In one or two cases I have permanently reduced the rent by paying the tithe	I believe the estate was valued in 1863. Rents have not been raised on sitting tenants. On fresh takings there has been sometimes a small increase, but generally on account of some improvement executed by me

MONMOUTHSHIRE.

Name and Address of Landowner	Estate	Abatements	Reductions	Observations as to the History of Rents
C. Bosanquet. Dingestow Court, Monmouth	Dingestow (2580 acres)	10 p.c. on rents due February 1878 to February 1880, inclusive; 20 p.c. on rents due August 1880; some 10, some 20 p.c. on rents due February 1881; 10 p.c. on *reduced* rents due August 1885 to August 1888 inclusive; 5 p.c. on rents due February and August 1889; 10 p.c. on rents due August 1892	The rents were reduced in 1881 for the most part, but some before — *i.e.*, about 1879 — and some since. The reduction amounts to rather more than 29 p.c., viz., from £2231 in 1877 to £1574 in 1892	—
J. A. Bradney. Tal-y-coed Court	Tal-y-coed (1500 acres)	—	On most of the farms the rents have been permanently reduced, so much so that no abatement has since been applied for by any tenant, and none has been given. Most of the farms have been purchased since 1880	—
Rev. J. T. Harding. Pentwyn, Rockfield Monmouth	Pentwyn and Deepholme (200 acres)	I am giving back now 10 p.c. on a reduced rental	Since 1877 rents have been reduced 30 p.c.	When I purchased Deepholme in 1873 I found the tenant leaving of his own accord, and I re-let at a 10 p.c. higher rent than he had been paying, and had no difficulty in so doing. That rent has been reduced as stated

Capt. Homfray, Penllyn Castle, Cowbridge	Penllyn Castle. (In Glamorgan and Monmouth 2025 acres)	Abatements of 5 to 10 p.c. have been made; for the last audit rent 15 p.c.	Since 1877 some reductions have been made in the case of old tenants	The estate has not been re-valued within the last 50 years, nor have rents been raised
J. Lawrence, Caerleon House	1500 acres	I have granted several abatements since 1877, but not uniformly, as most of my property is occupied by tenants under leases	I have in two instances granted a permanent reduction of from 15 to 20 p.c. where leases were running and the term unexpired. In two other instances my tenants have sold the unexpired term of their leases, in the one case for £110, and in the other for £80; and in a third case, where the lease had to run about 20 years, the tenant in possession sold the unexpired term for *six hundred pounds*	—
Sir W. T. Lewis, The Mardy, Aberdare	In Brecon, Glamorgan, Carmarthen, and Monmouth (1200 acres)	—	A farm in Monmouthshire, purchased by me in 1886, was held by the tenant under an agreement, dated June 1866, at a rental of £246 per annum, but this had been reduced by verbal arrangement prior to my purchase to £239 per annum; and, although I have, since the purchase, spent over £400 on the farm buildings, the tenant has been granted a lease for 14 years at the reduced rent	I have only acquired the farms within the last 20 years, and there has been no re-valuation since they have come into my possession; neither have the rents been raised

MONMOUTHSHIRE—(*continued*).

Name and Address of Landowner	Estate	Abatements	Reductions	Observations as to the History of Rents
Lord Llangattock The Hendre	The Hendre (5000 acres)	On eleven occasions since 1877 abatements of from 10 p.c. to 50 p.c. have been granted	Since 1877 permanent reductions amounting to about 25 p.c. have been made	The estate has not been revalued in the last half-century, nor have rents been raised
Major R. H. Mansel (as trustee for Mrs. Mansel and his own property)	In Monmouth, Glamorgan, and Brecon. (500 acres)	Abatements have been granted of 5, 6½, 17, 9, 10 and 8 p.c.	—	The estate has not been revalued
Mrs. Perry-Herrick, Beau Manor Park, Loughborough	Pen Coed and Penhow. (4120 acres)	Some farms have been kept at the original rent (on the rent-roll); these have had allowances since 1877, viz.: 1877, 10 p.c.; 1878, 10 p.c.; 1879, 30 p.c.; 1880, 15 p.c.; 1881, 10 p.c.; 1882, 10 p.c.; 1883, 10 p.c.; 1884, 12½ p.c.; 1885, 15 p.c.; 1886, 15 p.c.; 1887, 35 p.c.; 1888, 35 p.c. (from this year permanently reduced 20 p.c.); and in 1892 abatement 20 p.c. on reduced rent. Other farms reduced since 1877, permanent reductions made according to circumstances	The rent-roll of farming lands (1877) was £4827 11s.; in 1892, £4355 18s. 4d. (with increased acreage of about 300 acres). The rental shows that returns and abatements to tenants from 1877 to 1892 amount to £7142 7s. 3d. outside of reduced rents	The estate has not been revalued within the last 50 years. Rents have certainly not been raised during that period

Trustees of the Trellech Charity Lands	23 acres	12 p.c. was granted on one year to one tenant; and 8 p.c. was granted on one year to another tenant	One holding has been reduced from £12 to £10.	One holding near Monmouth has been raised from £10 to £12 per annum, but we have had £480 offered for this holding, which shows that we have been receiving only 2½ p.c. on this land and tenement, and have been liable for all repairs also
Mrs. Tudor Wyesham House, Dixton	Wyesham and Llanolway. (330 acres)	An abatement has been granted since 1878 of £6 per annum to one of three tenants at Llanolway. This year 10 p.c.	Since 1877 I should say the rents have been permanently reduced 30 p.c.	The estate was re-valued in 1884 resulting in a great reduction of rents
Geo. Willis Newton Hall, Dixton	Cwm-Collier farm (110 acres)	—	In 1889 I reduced the rent 33 p.c., and it has so continued since	—

PEMBROKESHIRE.

Rev. Canon Allen Porthkerry, Barry	Blackalden (in Pembroke and Carmarthen, 750 acres)	I have made abatements from 4 to 7½ p.c. in bad years	No. All are to the best of my knowledge and belief reasonably low	—
George Baugh Allen Albert Terrace, Regent's Park	Cilrhiw. (580 acres)	March 25, 1880, 5 p.c.; September 29, 1885, 15 p.c.; March 25, 1886, 15 p.c.; September 29, 1886, 15 p.c.; March 26, 1887, 10 p.c.; September 29, 1887, 10 p.c.; March 25, 1888, 10 p.c.; September 29, 1888, 10 p.c.; March 25, 1889, 10 p.c.; September 29, 1891, 15 p.c.; March 25, 1892, 15 p.c.; September 29, 1892, 20 p.c.	I have not since 1877 permanently reduced any rents	There has been no increase in rent for 50 years, with the exception of a slight increase from £223 to £275 on the expiration of a 30 years' lease following on a 20 years' lease

PEMBROKESHIRE—*(continued)*.

Name and Address of Landowner	Estate	Abatements	Reductions	Observations as to the History of Rents
Hy. George Allen, Q.C. Paskeston, Pembroke	Paskeston (440 acres)	Abatements have been granted on half-yearly rents (not uniform) ranging from 10 to 20 p.c. I think nearer the latter amount	Permanent reductions, since I bought the property at the close of 1879, have been made, which reduced the rental from £530 to £426	—
James Bevan Bowen, Llwyngwair	Llwyngwair (in Pembroke, Cardigan, and Carmarthen, 3303 acres)	In 1885, 1886, 1887, and 1888, I returned 10 p.c. to tenants; in 1891, 5 p.c., and in 1892, 10 p.c.	In 1885 I reduced 15 p.c. on two large farms permanently, and again in 1890 on another farm because the tenants depended so much on corn, the lands being dry and less adapted for permanent pasture than most of the land in the Pembrokeshire district	I came into the estate in 1856 (37 years ago), and am not aware of any increase of rent during the preceding 12 years. There has been no increase since
Thomas Harman Brenchley, Glancirw, Cardigan	Farms in the parish of Dogmaels	From July 1886 to January 1888 I gave 7½ p.c.; in 1889, 5 p.c.; January 1893, 5 p.c.	In 1880 I reduced rent of principal farm £30 per annum, from £270 to £240	—
Mrs. Briestocke, Blaenpant, Bancrath	Blaenpant (in Pembrokeshire and Cardiganshire, 4500 acres)	In 1879, 10 p.c. from the Michaelmas rents; in 1881, 10 p.c. from the Michaelmas rents; and from 1885 to the present time, 10 p.c. from every half-year's rent	I have permanently reduced the rents of three farms, one to the extent of £50 a year; another £15 and another £5	The estate has never been revalued as a whole. There have been some increase of rent on change of tenancy

Mrs. Brook . The Croft, Tenby	Ivy Tower (between 900 and 1000 acres)	In 1886, 1687, and 1888, 10 p.c.; 1889, 5 p.c.; 1892, 10 p.c.—in a few cases, 5 p.c.	I have not permanently reduced any rents since 1877	Part of the estate has been valued within the last 50 years, and is now let on that valuation
Earl of Cawdor . Stackpole Court, Pembroke	Stackpole, Wiston, Walton and Burton. (In Pembroke, Carmarthen, and Cardigan, 70,000 acres)	For three years from Lady Day 1885, to Lady Day 1886, allowances of 15 p.c. were made to the farm tenants. For one year, from Lady Day 1891, the tithes have been allowed being about 7½ p.c. For the present year, from Lady Day 1892, the tithes are again allowed, and an additional 10 p.c. out of the rents	No permanent reduction of rents of any consequence up to the present time. Now a few trifling reductions are proposed	All the estates were valued about 30 years back; and the rents were increased by re-lettings, about £5000 a year
Major J. V. Colby Rhosygilwen, Boncath	Fynone. (In Pembroke and Carmarthen, about 10,000 acres)	In 1886, 10 p.c. was allowed; in 1887, 10 p.c.; first half-year of 1888, 10 p.c.; second half-year of 1888, 5 p.c.; last half-year of 1891, 10 p.c.; last half-year of 1892, 10 p.c.	Reductions have been made in a few cases where farms were purchased with high rentals. The rental of the original estate has not been altered for several generations	In the last 50 years there has been no re-valuation; nor have rents been raised
Baron de Rutzen Slebech Park, Haverfordwest	Slebech. (5000 acres)	I have returned 10 p.c. for the last two half-years	I only succeeded to the estate about three years ago, and have only permanently reduced the rent of one farm since	The estate has not been re-valued during the last 50 years, nor have rents been raised in the period
Erasmus Gower, Castle Malgwyn, Boncath	Clynderwen, Gilanda van, Castle Malgwyn. (In Pembrokeshire and Carmarthenshire, 2360 acres)	1890, Lady Day, 5 p.c.; 1891, Lady Day, 5 p.c.; Michaelmas, 5 p.c.; 1892, Lady Day, 10 p.c., Michaelmas, 5 p.c.	I succeeded in 1884, and have made reductions of 6 p.c. on two farms	Rents have not been raised to my knowledge during the last 25 years, except on one farm held on a 21 years' lease expired in 1885. In this case the tenant sub-let about half the farm for £1 less than the total rent. Most of the sub-tenants have continued on their holdings, and the remainder of the land is let as a separate farm

PEMBROKESHIRE—(continued).

Name and Address of Landowner	Estate	Abatements	Reductions	Observations as to the History of rents
Major Parry Hughes and Mrs. Hughes, Allt-Lwyd, Aberystwith	Allt-Lwyd and Mabws. (In Cardiganshire and Pembrokeshire, 3500 acres)	In some cases 5 p.c.	All rents have been permanently reduced. Some instances: Farm, £110 per annum for 50 years, reduced to £90 present rent; farm, £180 per annum for 50 years, reduced to £130 present rent; farm, £290 per annum for 40 years, reduced to £230 present rent; and other farms have been reduced £10 and £5 per annum. These farms are upon the Allt-Lwyd estate corn land, and were let by my father about 45 years since. No rents have been raised by me	The Allt-Lwyd estate was re-valued five years since; the old rents were reduced 15 p.c.
Edward Laws, Tenby	(800 acres)	I have granted abatements of 10 p.c. in 1891, and 15 p.c. in 1892	—	—
Henry Leach, Corston, Near Pembroke	Corston. (1800 acres)	Abatements have been made in a few cases only	Since 1877 rents have been reduced, though only in a few cases, about 10 p.c.	The rents, except in a very few cases of new lettings have not been altered for 50 years, possibly much longer. The estate has never to my knowledge been re-valued (or rental, as a whole, within the

| Mrs. Lewis, Boneath Clynfiew | Clynfiew. (In Pembroke, Cardigan, and Carmarthen, 4870 acres) | Abatements have twice been granted. 10 p.c. was given on the rents payable Michaelmas 1885, and Michaelmas 1892. Reductions have frequently been made at other times during this interval in *individual cases* | A slight reduction has been made in the case of two farms, £5 a year each. | The estate has not been re-valued *for purposes of rental*, but in 1888 a competent local valuer went over the whole property for the purpose of inspecting the state of repair and cultivation; of re-arranging boundaries, and re-adjusting values where necessary. The estate was at that time very unequally let, and the valuer advised a reduction in some cases and an increase in others. His recommendations were followed, but the rents were not raised to the figures mentioned by him in any one case, and in many cases no change was made at all. The net result of the valuation was a slight increase of the estate rental | last 50 years, I have, at different times, had valuations made for my own information, but not with a view of altering rents. The valuations in all cases exceed the rentals, some as much as 20 p.c. |

PEMBROKESHIRE—(continued).

Name and Address of Landowner	Estate	Abatements	Reductions	Observations as to the History of Rents
Bishop of Llandaff .	Henllan Grove. (In Pembroke and Carmarthen, 3500 acres)	In 1886, 1887, 1888, and 1892, I returned 10 p.c. I succeeded to the properties in the year 1886	Since 1886 I have made reductions in eight instances on the Henllan estate, amounting to the annual sum of £115. On the Grove estate reductions have been made in six instances amounting to the annual sum of £120	The estate has not been revalued for the last 50 years as far as I am aware. I have not raised the rent in any single instance since I became possessed of the estates
Thos. Edward Lloyd Coedmore, near Cardigan	Coedmore and Trewern. (In Cardigan, Carmarthen, and Pembroke, 4500 acres)	For the Coedmore estate 5 p.c. was allowed at Lady Day 1886, Michaelmas 1886; Lady Day and Michaelmas 1887; Lady Day and Michaelmas 1888, and Lady Day 1889; and for Michaelmas 1892, 10 p.c. (except where there were leases). For the Trewern estate, 10 p.c. allowed at Michaelmas 1865, and Lady Day 1886; the same at Lady Day and Michaelmas 1887; the same at Lady Day and Michaelmas 1888; 5 p.c. was allowed at Lady Day 1889, and 10 p.c. at Michaelmas 1892	Since 1887 rents have not been reduced very materially	The Trewern estate was revalued in the year 1864, for the purpose of a partition between my late mother and Mr. Longcroft of Llanina, Cardiganshire, and such valuation has not been materially altered since that period, except in cases where old leases have fallen in

Frederick Lewis Lloyd Phillips, Pen y Park, Haverfordwest	Pen y Park (2255 acres)	Abatements were made in 1887 and 1888 of 5 p.c., and in 1892 of 10 p.c.	No reductions have been made	The estate has not been re-valued, nor have rents been raised during the last 50 years
Henry Mathias, 13 Hill Street, Haverfordwest	Cornel Bach, Middle Hook, Pontslarn meadow, &c., Scarrow Scant. (145 acres)	I have made no abatement; nothing has been asked except 10 tons of lime, which I gave the tenant of a farm three or four years after I purchased it	When I purchased the Scarrow Scant fields, they were (together with the cottage thereon) let at £36 a year, and I continued to receive that rent down to Michaelmas 1890, when the tenant gave up the fields, having taken a larger extent of land in the county of Pembroke. From Michaelmas 1890, the rent has been reduced to £29, the actual reduction being £7. The tithe rent-charge, about £2, is paid by myself	The estate has not to my knowledge been re-valued
R. W. B. Mirehouse, Angle, Pembroke	Angle. (3000 acres)	In 1886, 1887, and 1888, I allowed 15 p.c. abatement; in 1889, 10 p.c. abatement; in 1890, 5 p.c. abatement; in 1892, 10 p.c. abatement; in 1893, 15 p.c. abatement	—	The estate was re-valued about 1879. There has been a moderate increase of rent in a few cases
Rev. Thos. Gwynne Mortimer, The Court, Llanllawer, Fishguard	The Court, Llanllawer. (800 acres)	No abatements in money, but I have made many improvements such as buildings, &c, and have given manure in some cases. This year I give manure (amounting to about £8 p.c.) to all. My rents are unusually low	I have not permanently reduced any of my rents. I have intimated that if any of the occupiers would like a fresh valuation I should be willing	The estate has not been re-valued

PEMBROKESHIRE—*(continued)*.

Name and Address of Landowner	Estate	Abatements	Reductions	Observations as to the History of Rents
G. L. Owen and Mrs. Owen Withybush, Haverfordwest	Kingston, Parish of St. Michael, (1900 acres)	I have granted abatements of 10 p.c. in 1886, 1887, 1888, and 1892	I have not reduced any rents	The rents were arranged on the purchase of the estate in 1857 by the father of the present owners. They have not been altered since
Judge Owen Ty Gwyn, Abergavenny	Withybush, Poyston, Honeybrook Farm. (1541 acres)	Abatements have been given in the years 1886, 1887, and 1889, of 10 p.c.; in 1890, Lady Day rents, 10 p.c.; Michaelmas rents, 15 p.c.	I have reduced some rents. The deductions amount to about £133 a year	This property has been in the possession of my family for more than 50 years. During that time the rents have not been raised, and in some cases are 20 p.c. lower at present than they have been, although large sums of money have been spent on new buildings and repairs
Edward Perkins Penugwarne, Fishguard	In Pembrokeshire (800 acres)	Gave an abatement of 10 p.c. all round last half-year's audit	Have reduced some of the highest rented land by 10 p.c.	Rents have certainly been raised during the last 50 years; in some cases doubled, and even then the tenants have saved enough to buy their farms
Edward Picton Phillips Haverfordwest	Kilbarth and South-lays. (432 acres)	I have never been asked to grant abatements	I have not permanently reduced my rents	About 10 years ago the estate was re-valued. In the opinion of the valuer I should have been justified in raising the value per acre 15s., in

Mrs. Lort Phillips and John Fredk. Lort Phillips, Lawrenny Park, Pembroke	Lawrenny, Nash and Llanstadwell. (6500 acres)	In 1885 the rents were reduced to what they were prior to 1854, date of the Russian war, considered to be the worst period in agriculture	In some few cases since 1887 rents have been permanently reduced	steal of the present value, 10s. 6d. I declined to do so; the rents therefore remain the same as during the last 50 years
Miss Prothero, Norton, Tenby	Loveston. (465 acres)	I granted abatements in 1885, 1886, and 1887, and again in 1891, 1892, and 1893, having returned a percentage of 15 p.c.	Previous to 1888 I reduced the rents of two of my tenants—one from £191 to £175, and another from £85 to £65	The estate was re-valued in 1876, resulting in an increase of about £600 per annum
Wm. H. Richards, Croft House, Tenby	Croft House (650 acres)	During the depressed years I have allowed certain of my tenants on an average 10 p.c.	I have not since 1887 made any permanent reductions, the greater portion having been held on lease	My property in 1836, let for £354 per annum; in 1892 it was let for £310 per annum, from which it will be seen that my rents are less now than they were in 1838, and in addition to this I have made considerable allowances, and laid out large sums in repairs
John Reynolds, Treglennis, Croscoch, Letterston	Treglennis (350 acres)	—	I have reduced rent from £60 to £50	—

PEMBROKESHIRE—(continued).

Name and Address of Landowner	Estate	Abatements	Reductions	Observations as to the History of Rents
Edward Schaw-Protheroe, Dol-Wilym	Dol - Wilym and Killerwin. (In Carmarthenshire and Pembroke, 1600 acres)	Abatements have been made in bad years, 1882, 1885, 1886, 1887, and 1888, to about 5 or 6 p.c. In 1892 the tithe-rent charge was remitted on a part of the estate for the year, and on the remainder for the half-year	In 1882 I reduced the rent of the largest farm 10 p.c., having granted a lease of 21 years not long before	The history of this small property is shortly this: In my grandfather's time farms were held on leases of three lives, and these fell in in my mother's time, who succeeded in 1841, and the farms were then re-valued. I succeeded in 1872. The only lease of lives fell in soon after, and that farm was then re-valued. I have since reduced it by 10 p.c.
A.P. Saunders-Davies, Pentre, Boncath	Pentre. (In Pembroke, Cardigan and Carmarthen, 6700 acres)	No abatements	In one case the rent of a farm was reduced from £90 to £80	The Pentre Old estate was re-valued about 30 years ago. Some of the farms were increased in rental and some reduced. The Pentre (Twindeg) estate was bought in 1884, and the rents have remained the same with the addition of the tithe
Colonel Saurin, Orielton, Pembroke	Orielton, (5582 acres)	1887, 10 p.c. to yearly tenants; 1888, 5 p.c. to leaseholders; 7½ p.c. to yearly tenants; 5 p.c. to leaseholders. 1892 (on half-year's rent due Michaelmas), 15 p.c. to yearly tenants and leaseholders	The permanent reduction since 1887 on certain farms to about £165	The estate has not been re-valued, neither have rents been raised within the last 26 years, when it came into possession of my family

| Wm. Stancomb, Blount's Court, Potterne, Devizes | 1500 acres | I have often granted abatements on occasion of bad seasons and other circumstances previous to 1886 (from that time a permanent reduction) and intend granting a further abatement owing to the increased depression. On my Southwood property I made an abatement from 1885 to 1892 of £708 15s.; from 1887 to 1892 of £389 12s. 4d. On my Folkestone and other property I made an abatement from 1869 to 1892 of £353 13s. 6d.; from 1877 to 1892 of £282 14s. 4d. | I permanently reduced my rents 20 p.c. from 1886 | No rents have been raised since I have had possession from 1854 |
| Hon. R. C. and Hon. Mrs. Trollope, Crowcombe Court, Taunton | Carew | I have granted abatements of 10 p.c. from 1884 to 1889, and again 10 p.c. from 1892 | — | No rents have been raised that I know of, except in the cases of leases on lives falling in, where, instead of paying a fine, the land has been let at a fair rent, on a yearly tenancy |

GLAMORGANSHIRE.

Name and Address of Landowner	Estate	Abatements	Reductions	Observations as to the History of Rents
A. C. Bruce Pryce, Abertholme, Cheltenham	Monknash, near Bridgend. (3100 acres)	In 1882 we returned the tenants 5 p.c. on the agricultural farms	In the same year, as the decline of prices of produce seemed likely to last, the estate was re-valued, and the rents reduced on an average of about 10 p.c. In 1886 there was a further reduction on one large farm, and again, in 1889, there were further reductions, so that the total rents (including tithes), which in 1878 were £2377, are now £1850, equal to a reduction of 25 p.c.	The whole estate was re-valued in 1873, and that re-valuation increased the rents about 7¼ p.c. The Monknash Estate was re-valued in 1882, and the rents reduced as I have mentioned
Marquis of Bute, Cardiff Castle	Glamorganshire Estate. (22,000 acres)	No, except in one or two exceptional cases not referable to agricultural depression	No, except in one or two exceptional cases	The estate has not been re-valued as a whole within the last 50 years. Rents have not been raised except in one or two instances under very exceptional circumstances
Godfrey L. Clark, Talygarn, and Mrs. Jackson, Manor House, Dawlish, in moieties	The Heath Estate. (2745 acres in Glamorgan principally and Monmouth)	Percentages have been allowed during the years 1879, 1886, 1887, 1888, and 1889, and when wanted by the tenant time has been given for payment	No permanent reduction has been made	The estate was re-valued in 1872, but the variation in rental was small

D. H. Davies, Morfa House, Llantwit Major, Cowbridge	107 acres	Reduced 20 p.c. since 1877	—	I did not succeed to the property until 1874. I believe this property was advanced 10 p.c. in the year 1857. The tenant at this rent—that is, something less than £1 per acre—gets on fairly well
Frederick Lewis Davis, Abergavenny	Rhoose Farm, near Cowbridge. (194 acres)	No	About the year 1880 my father reduced the rent from £250 to £200 a year, making a reduction of 20 p.c. permanently	The rent of this farm has not been altered for 60 years, with the exception of the reduction of 20 p.c. referred to
Earl of Dunraven, Dunraven Castle, Bridgend	Dunraven Estate (24,000 acres)	Abatements of rent commenced being made in the year, February and Lady Day 1885, to February and Lady Day 1886, and have continued every year to the present time, at the rate of 15 and 10 p.c., according to the circumstances of the case, the great majority at 15 p.c.	In some cases, not many, a permanent reduction has been made	The estate was valued by an independent valuer in 1887 for purposes of rental. His valuation exceeded the rents charged by over 8 p.c., but the valuation was not put in force
Mrs. Gwyn, Dyffryn, Neath	Dyffryn. (3510 acres)	Yes, frequently; amounts of 10 p.c., 15 p.c., and 20 p.c. have been remitted to individual tenants, leaseholders, as well as yearly tenants. 10 p.c. all round was remitted at the last rent audit	Yes, many of the rents have been permanently reduced. During the last 12 years, ending September 29th, 1892, the rental of the Glamorganshire Estate has been reduced about 8 p.c. all round	There has been no re-valuation of the estate
Captain J. G. R. Homfray, Penllyn Castle, Cowbridge	Penllyn Castle Estate. (2025 acres in Glamorgan and Monmouth)	Yes, from 5 p.c. to 10 p.c.; for the last rent audit, 15 p.c.	Yes, some in the case of old tenants	The estate has not been re-valued, nor have rents been raised during the last 50 years

GLAMORGANSHIRE—(continued).

Name and Address of Landowner	Estate	Abatements	Reductions	Observations as to the History of Rents
O. H. Jones, Fonmon Castle, Cowbridge	Fonmon Castle (1100 acres)	Yes, regularly every year. Since 1879 the amounts vary from 5 to 20 p.c. on different farms and at different times	Yes, on two farms, about 12 p.c.	The estate has not been re-valued. Rents were raised in some instances by my late father, I think, about 1870
James Lewis, Plas Draw, Aberdare	Llwydcoed. (1800 acres in Glamorganshire and Brecknockshire)	10 p.c. for the last 7 years, excepting in 1889-90, and 15 p.c. for the half-year ending August 1892	No	—
Sir William Thomas Lewis, The Mardy, Aberdare	Glamorganshire. (1200 acres in Brecknockshire, Glamorganshire, Carnarvonshire, and Monmouthshire)	(Abatements in Breconshire)	Reduction in Monmouthshire	I have only acquired the farms within the last 20 years, and there has been no re-valuation since they have come into my possession, nor have rents been raised during that time
Mrs. Mackintosh of Mackintosh, Cottrell	Llancaiach Estate (held in equal moieties with Edward Rhys Wingfield, Esq.), also separate estates at Cottrell and Taffswell. (5025 acres)	No abatement on Llancaiach Estate. A rebate of 10 p.c. made to Cottrell Estate tenants last audit	No. Cottrell Estate was only acquired in 1891, when it was valued	The estate has not been re-valued. The rents are practically the same as they were 50 years ago

| Major Robert Henry Mansel, as trustee for Mrs. I. A. Mansel and own property | Glamorganshire (130 acres) | Yes, 5 p.c., 6½ p.c., 17 p.c., 9 p.c., 10 p.c., 8 p.c. (*See* statement sent by Major Mansel) | The estate has not been revalued, nor have rents been raised so far as I am aware |

MAJOR MANSEL'S PROPERTY.

AMOUNT OF RENTS RECEIVED FOR NARTEG ISHA FARM.

Rent received				Amount paid in Repairs			
	£	s.	d.		£	s.	d.
1886	15	0	0 half-year				
1887	30	0	0	Bill for Calves Cottage	7	0	0
1888	*25	0	0				
1889	25	0	0				
1890	25	0	0				
1891	27	13	8 } (These amounts include	Rees Morgan, repairs	1	6	8
1892	27	16	10 } tithes)	Wm. Daniel, jun., repairs	9	17	0
1893				A. J. Arnold & Co	14	16	3
	175	10	6		32	19	11

This farm is situate in the parish of Cilybebyll in Glamorganshire; it consists of a dwelling-house with suitable farm buildings and 130 acres of pasture land; from the above figures it will be seen that the rent inclusive of tithes amounts to about 4s. 6d. per acre. * Rent reduced. Tenant paid tithes until 1891.

N.B.—It will be seen that in the last seven years nearly 20 p.c. of the rent has been paid away in repairs.—R. H. M.

GLAMORGANSHIRE—(continued).

Name and Address of Landowner	Estate	Abatements	Reductions			Observations as to the History of Rents
John Cole Nicholl Merthyr Mawr	Merthyr Mawr (3154 acres)	Yes, 1879–1887 until the tenants: a special allowance to each tenant, not a general percentage, as the rents are very uneven. Some tenants with high rents get allowances every year, though their rents are nominally the same. Others get allowances frequently, while the very old takings seldom get allowances as the rents are low. Rents are never raised on the occupying tenants	Yes, by abatement continued year by year, or by permanent reduction whenever necessary			Estate has never been re-valued. I am told by tenant that one farm was re-valued and rent raised for selling purposes and never reduced. However, it is now particularly low-rented. The usual plan is to re-value farms on death of the tenant, and to re-let on that basis. The new rent is generally higher than the old one, as the old rents are below market value, in many cases being very old. This plan has not been invariably carried out. It is the rule never to raise the rent on the occupying tenant on this estate
			Farm	Old Rent	New Rent	
				£	£	
			Llanfia .	400	320	
			Clement and Bcors .	123	120	
			Wick .	90	80	
			Candlestone .	205	190	
			Witney .	210	190	
			Laleston .	44	32	
			Croesywtta .	180	150 [a]	
			Merthyr Mawr .	400	320	
			Pentrellwnt .	180	Annual allowance £15 per annum	
			Tyla .	110	Annual allowance £7 per annum	

a Further offer of a reduction of £16 per annum 1892

			See in "Abatements" column	
Thomas Penrice, Kilvrough, near Swansea	Kilvrough (5500 acres)	No substantial abatement has been made on this estate for the last 50 years, nor have the rents been raised to any appreciable extent	See in "Abatements" column	The last valuation of the estate was made nearly 50 years ago, and its effect was to equalise rather than to increase or reduce the rental. Rents have not been raised "to any appreciable extent" during the last 50 years
C. J. Collins Prichard, and Mrs. Prichard, 29 Victoria Sq., Clifton	Twllywrach, parish of Colwinstone. (900 to 1000 acres)	We only came into possession of the bulk of the estate since the latter end of 1878. Since 1878 abatements have been made to tenants varying from 5 to 15 p.c., and in one case the entire half-year's rent of one farm, £40, was given back, and this put the farmer on his legs	In 1889 a permanent reduction was made of 15 p.c.	We do not think the estate has been re-valued during the last 50 years. The Village Farm was slightly raised by the late owner. One farm, the Tydraw Farm, formerly let at 25s. an acre, is now let at 15s. an acre, including tithes
Lewis William Shedden, Craigwen, Lymington	Craigwen and Pontypandy. (430 acres)	I have never been asked to grant any abatements, or return any percentages	No, there has never been any occasion	The estate has not been revalued during the last 50 years. The rent of Craigwen Farm was raised £5 last year when it changed tenants, the out-going tenant having made sufficient money on the farm to retire
Sir Arthur Stepney, Bart.	The Stepney Estate. (About 180 acres in Glamorganshire)	10 p.c. allowance from rent during from March 25, 1845, to March 25, 1888. In the last 12 months of this period we also allowed the rates on the 10 p.c. since we have been giving in kind	—	A valuation, chiefly for private information, and which was not acted upon, was made in 1880, and on this small quantity of land in Glamorganshire the valuation showed an increase of about 12 p.c.

GLAMORGANSHIRE—(*continued*).

Name and Address of Landowner	Estate	Abatements	Reductions	Observations as to the History of Rents
Miss Talbot. Margam Park	Margam and Gower (13692 acres)	In 1892, 15 p.c.; in 1886, 25 p.c.; and in 1881, 20 p.c.	In very few cases. The total reduction would not exceed £150 a year on the Margam estate. In Gower none of any consequence	The estate has not been re-valued, but during the last 36 years there has been a re-vision of the rent in every case of a new tenancy. Rents have been raised in a great many cases when a change of tenancy has taken place, but only then. Until 1858 there was hardly any change, but from that time until 1880 there was an increase in the rent when the circumstances would admit. In Gower the raising of rent on change of tenancy has not uncommonly been the result of competition among applicants
Colonel Turberville. Ewenny Priory	Ewenny Priory (3000 acres)	To my knowledge for the last 9 years half of all local rates have been remitted, and generally 5 p.c. in addition; also during the last 6 or 7 years the landlord has paid all the tithes, which have never been added to the rent, making the total annual de-duction 15 to 20 p.c.	One farm in the parish of Mar-cross, over 6 p.c. Copy of letter, June 24 : "The average yearly sum ex-pended in repairs and im-provements on farms on above estate for 12 years ending March 31, 1893, was £272 13s. 4d., or 10·4 p.c. on net rental of £2500. For many years past there has been allowed off the rents all the tithe and half of the rates. Rentals are a little below the valuation"	The estate has not been re-valued to my knowledge, nor have I heard of its being done. In the parish of Ewenny, wherein the estate mostly lies, there was a valua-tion made for rating purposes in 1872, the gross estimated rental of which was used for rating purposes from which the deductions specified have been used

John Edw. Vaughan. Rheola	Rheola Estate. (5800 acres in Glamorgan and Brecon)	On occasions abatements have been made in individual cases, but no general abatement has been made, the rents having remained unaltered for a very long period	The rent-roll from farms on this estate is about 4 p.c. lower than it was in 1877, and in some cases the lands are let tithe free, which increases the percentage of reduction by about another 2 p.c., making in all 6 p.c. reduction	There has been no general valuation of the property during the period named. A considerable portion of it had been let at nominal rents for lives by a former owner, a fine having been taken, and as these fell in from 1823 to 1858, the farms were re-let at fair rents. Except in a few instances there has since then been little variation
A. V. H. Vaughan-Lee Dillington Park, Ilminster	Llanllay. (5800 acres in Glamorgan and Brecknockshire)	No general reduction or abatement has been made, but in some instances allowances have been made. 10 p.c. was allowed to the tenants in Llangyfelach parish at the Christmas collection	Taking the whole of the farm rental it is 7 p.c. less now than in 1877	No general re-valuation has taken place, but in some instances rents have been altered. Comparing the rental of a portion of the property (about 3500 acres) the difference in the rental between the present time and 50 years ago is £44 10s. in favour of the present time. Taking the area above quoted the difference in rental as between the present time and 50 years ago, is less than 4 p.c. In some individual cases the rent is the same, and in some cases lower. The difference chiefly arises from one farm, the rent of which in 1843 was £137 10s., and at the present £200 tithe free. This farm was let from 1865 to 1882 for £250. It is possible that in 1843 an old lease existed, but this I cannot trace

GLAMORGANSHIRE—(continued).

Name and Address of Landowner	Estate	Abatements	Reductions	Observations as to the History of Rents
Lord Windsor . Cardiff	Windsor (18,187 acres)	In 1879, 10 p.c. on one year's rent. In 1881, 10 p.c. on half-year's rent : in 1886, 10 p.c. on one year's rent ; in 1887, 10 p.c. on one year's rent : In 1888, 10 p.c. on one year's rent ; in 1889, 10 p.c. on half-year's rent ; in 1892, 10 p.c. on half-year's rent	There has been no general reduction of rent, but rents have been reduced in special cases, the total permanent reduction amounting to £739 10s. As against this there have been increases on farms close to Cardiff in four instances. One farm of about 400 acres (the tenant of which retired, and whose family have occupied the farm since 1806) is now let principally as accommodation land, at an average of £2 per acre, which shows an increase on the rental of £423 10s. Another small holding, on change of tenancy (the old tenant having died) is now let as a dairy farm with improved buildings, shows an increase of £26 15s. Another farm shows a small increase of £28 15s., made on change of tenancy (the former tenant's family held the farm for a great number of years, at a low rent). The fourth	Estate has not been re-valued

Mrs. Johnes, Lieut.-General Sir J. Hills-Johnes, K.C.B., V.C., and Lady Hills-Johnes Dolaucothy	Dolaucothy. (3613 acres in Carmarthen and Glamorgan)	Lady Day 1882, on all the estates, 10 p.c. Michaelmas 1862, 10 p.c. to small tenants who pay once a year. 1883, 5 p.c. in Glamorganshire. 1884, 5 p.c. in Glamorganshire. 1885, 8 p.c. in Glamorganshire. Michaelmas 1885, 10 p.c. on all estates. Lady Day 1886, 10 p.c. on all estates. Michaelmas 1886, 10 p.c. on all estates. Lady Day and Michaelmas 1887, 10 p.c. on all estates. Lady Day 1888, 10 p.c. on all estates. Lady Day and Michaelmas 1892, 10 p.c. on all estates	case being an increase of £12 for exceedingly good house and buildings erected, the tenant requiring this, being a land agent and valuer, and not dependent on the farm for a living. The net decrease, notwithstanding the increase before mentioned, amounts since 1877 to £248 11s. £ s. d. Rents reduced . 155 13 0 " increased . 13 10 0 142 3 0	Estates have not been re-valued. Some of the rents have been raised, probably due to re-adjustment of land or to rebuilding of the farm-house and out-buildings. Every farm-house and its out-buildings has been put into thorough order, many re-built
Colonel Gould Frampton	Great Frampton (160 acres)	I allowed an abatement in the years 1882, 1883, 1884, of ten p.c.	25 p.c. From £300 to £225, beginning in 1885	—
Mrs. Booker Velindra House, Cardiff	Velindra and Maesmawr. (547 acres)	Not required	It was re-valued in 1885, the result being to reduce my receipt	—

GLAMORGANSHIRE—(continued).

Name and Address of Landowner	Estate	Abatements	Reductions	Observations as to the History of Rents
Miss Clara Thomas, Llwyn Madoc, Garth	Llanbeadarch (1152 acres)	The following abatements have been made:—1886, 10 p.c. 1887, 10 p.c. Half-year ending February 1888, 10 p.c. Half-year ending August, 1892, 10 p.c. Half-year ending February 1893, 10 p.c.	The rent roll has been reduced from £596 in 1874 to £537 in 1893	—

CARMARTHENSHIRE.

Name and Address of Landowner	Estate	Abatements	Reductions	Observations as to the History of Rents
George Baugh Allen, London	Cilrhiw. (In Carmarthenshire, 162 acres)	Abatements granted to agricultural tenants all round; March 25, 1880, 5 p.c.: September 29, 1885, 15 p.c.: March 25, 1886, 15 p.c.: September 29, 1886, 15 p.c.: March 25, 1887, 10 p.c.: September 29, 1887, 10 p.c.: March 25, 1888, 10 p.c.: September 29, 1888, 10 p.c.: March 25, 1889, 10 p.c.: September 29, 1891, 15 p.c.: March 25, 1892, 15 p.c.: September 29, 1892, 20 p.c.	No reductions	In 1876 there was a slight increase from £223 10s. to £275 on expiration of a 30 years' lease, following on a 21 years' lease, there having been no increase for 50 years

Rev. Canon Allen Porthkerry, Barry	In Pembroke and Carmarthen (750 acres)	I have made abatements varying from 4 to 7½ p.c. in bad years	No; all are, to the best of my knowledge and belief, reasonably low	About the year 1850 I raised the rent on the Carmarthenshire farms about 25 p.c. on the termination of old leases
R. E. Arden Burnham, Slough	In Pembroke and Carmarthen (6250 acres)	10 p.c. at Michaelmas 1888; 10 p.c. at Lady Day 1892 to Michaelmas 1893, both inclusive	I have made no reductions since 1887	No valuation has been made within the last 30 years
Earl of Ashburnham, 30 Dover Street, W.	Pembrey and Llanddensant (7520 acres)	In 1886, 15 p.c. on one half-year's rent; in 1887-8, 15 p.c. on two half-years' rents; in 1889 on one half-year's rent; in 1892, 5 p.c. in January and 10 p.c. in July; in 1893, 10 p.c.	On the Pembrey estate rents have been reduced by about 14 p.c., but it is right to say that as some of these reductions were caused by the destruction of the land in consequence of the encroachment of the blowing sands from the seashore, the amount for the purposes of this investigation may be set at about 10½ p.c.	The Llanddensant estates were re-valued about 20 years ago, and the rents considerably increased, but it has never been regarded as a highly rented property
Edward H. Bath Alltyferin, Carmarthen	Alltyferin (1300 acres)	Michaelmas 1879, 5 p.c.; Michaelmas 1885, 20 p.c.; Lady Day 1886, 10 p.c.; Michaelmas 1886, 10 p.c.; Lady Day 1887, 10 p.c.; Michaelmas 1887, 10 p.c.; Lady Day 1888, 5 p.c.; Michaelmas 1889, 5 p.c.; Michaelmas 1891, half-year's tithes; Lady Day 1892, 7½ p.c.; Michaelmas 1892, 10 p.c.; Lady Day 1893, 15 p.c.; Michaelmas 1893, 10 p.c.	No	The estate was valued about 28 years ago, with the result of increasing the rental slightly

APPENDIX.

CARMARTHENSHIRE—(continued).

Name and Address of Landowner	Estate	Abatements	Reductions	Observations as to the History of Rents
His Honour Judge Bishop, Doly-garreg	Doly-garreg (1200 acres)	In the last year I have returned 10 p.c. to tenants.	I have not permanently reduced all the rents, but I have done so in two instances to a small amount	The estate has not been revalued, nor have rents been raised during the last 50 years
James Bevan-Bowen, Llwyngwair	Llwyngwair. (3203 acres in Pembroke, Cardigan, and Carmarthen)	In 1885, 6, 7 and 8 I returned 10 p.c. to tenants; also in 1891, 5 p.c., and in 1892, 10 p.c.	—	I came into the estate in 1856 (37 years ago) and am not aware of any increase of rent during the preceding 12 years. There has been no increase since.
H. S. Carver, Blaencorse, St. Clears	Blaencorse (300 acres)	10 p.c.	I have not reduced the rents since 1877	The rent of one farm has been raised at the expiration of an old lease : previously the rent was merely nominal.
Earl of Cawdor, Stackpole	Carmarthenshire. (70,000 acres in Pembroke, Carmarthen, and Cardigan)	For 3 years from Lady Day 1886 to Lady Day 1888, allowances of 15 p.c. were made to the farm tenants. For one year from Lady Day 1891 the tithes have been allowed, being almost 7½ p.c. For the present year from Lady Day 1892 the tithes are again allowed, and an additional 10 p.c. out of the rents	No permanent reductions of any consequence up to the present time. Now a few trifling reductions are proposed	All the estates were valued about 30 years back, and the rents were increased by re-lettings about £5000 a year

				The estate has not been revalued
Major Colby . . Ffynone	Ffynone. (10,000 acres in Pembroke and Carmarthen)	In 1886, 10 p.c. was allowed; in 1887, 10 p.c.; first half of 1888, 10 p.c.; second part of 1888, 5 p.c.; last half of 1891, 10 p.c.; last half of 1892, 10 p.c.	The rents have been reduced in a few cases where farms were purchased with high rentals. The rental of the original estate has not been altered for several generations	valued
Lord Dynevor . Dynevor Castle	Dynevor Castle (7000 acres)	10 p.c. on year's rent due Sept. 29, 1885; 10 p.c. on year's rent due Sept. 29, 1886; 10 p.c. on year's rent due Sept. 29, 1887; 10 p.c. on year's rent due March 25, 1892; 15 p.c. on year's rent due Sept. 29, 1892	A farm from . . £70 to 58 A farm from . . 68 to 52 A farm from . . 35 to 30 A farm from . . 15 to 38 A farm from . . 46 to 41 A farm from . . 82 to 80 A farm from . . 84 to 76 £130 to 375	The estate was re-valued in 1874, and the result was to increase receipts. Rents have been raised on re-lettings when they were extremely low let
L. G. De Ferry (jure uxoris) Kilymaenllwyd	Kilymaenllwyd (600 acres)	A percentage of 5 p.c. was returned to tenants at the two half-yearly rent audits in 1889; a percentage of 10 p.c. was returned to one particular tenant at the Michaelmas half-yearly audit in 1892	There have been no permanent reductions of rents since 1877	—
Erasmus Gower. Castle Malgwyn	Carmarthenshire. (2360 acres, in Pembroke and Carmarthen)	1890, Lady Day, 5 p.c.; 1891, Lady Day, 5 p.c.; 1891, Michaelmas, 5 p.c.; 1892, Lady Day, 10 p.c.; 1892, Michaelmas, 5 p.c.	I succeeded in 1884, and have made reductions of 6 p.c. on two farms	Rents have not been raised to my knowledge during the last 25 years, except on one farm held on a 21 years' lease expired in 1885

CARMARTHENSHIRE—(continued).

Name and Address of Landowner	Estate	Abatements	Reductions	Observations as to the History of Rents
Mrs. Gwyn Dyffryn, Neath	Blaen-awdde (1130 acres)	Amounts of 10 p.c., 15 p.c., and 20 p.c. have been remitted to individual tenants, lease-holders as well as yearly tenants. 10 p.c. all round was remitted at the last rent audit	Many of the rents have been permanently reduced. During the last 12 years ending September 29, 1892, the rental of the Carmarthen-shire estate has been remitted about 10 p.c. all round	The farm rents of the Carmarthen-shire estate were raised 4s. in the £ (i.e., 20 p.c.) by the late Mr. Howel Gwyn from Lady Day 1863 (30 years ago), 10 p.c. of which has now been permanently given back
Col. Gwynne-Hughes Glaneothy, Naugaredig	Glaneothy (800 acres)	In the years 1885 and 1886, 10 p.c. was granted; in the year 1887 7½ p.c. was granted	No permanent reduction has been made except in one case	There has been no valuation, though the rents have almost all been the same for the last 40 years
Edward Hopkins Carreg-Cennen, Llandilo	Carreg-Cennen	I have allowed 10 p.c. and 20 p.c. respectively since 1845, but there has been an intervening period when abatement was not wanted or expected	—	The estate has not been re-valued during the last 50 years
J. P. Howell Cardigan	Carmarthenshire, parish of Conwyl-Elfet. (311 acres)	In 1887 on the two half-years of 10 p.c.; also in 1892, and also I think intermediately on two or three occasions	I have reduced the rent of a small holding of house and fields from £12 10s. to £10	On one occasion I caused the estate to be re-valued; but the result was to leave it as it was, the rent neither increased nor reduced
Lt.-Col. W. P. Howell Penrhoel, Mydrym	Carmarthenshire (162 acres)	I have not till lately, then occasionally	No, because they have been rented low	—

P. L. Hughes-Garbett, Island House, Laugharne	Island House (650 acres)	At Lady Day 1893, 10 p.c.	No, except in one case to the extent of a few pounds only	The estate has not been re-valued: the rents remain about the same as in 1810, and have not been materially raised, while other lands neighbouring and of no better quality have paid largely increasing rents during the same period
R. E. Jennings, Gellideg, Kidwelly	Macnamara estate and other lands. (1013 acres)	1885, 10 p.c.; 1886, 20 p.c.; 1887, 15 p.c.; 1888, 7½ p.c.; 1891, 10 p.c. (at Michaelmas only); 1892, 10 p.c.	Rents have not since 1877 been permanently reduced	—
Mrs. Johnes, Lt.-Gen. Sir J. Hills-Johnes, K.C.B., V.C., and Lady Hills-Johnes, Dolaucothy	Dolaucothy. (3613 acres in Carmarthen and Glamorgan)	Lady Day 1882, 20 p.c.; Michaelmas 1882, 10 p.c. (to small tenants who pay once a year; Michaelmas 1885, 20 p.c.; Lady Day 1886, 10 p.c.; Michaelmas 1886, 10 p.c.; Lady Day and Michaelmas 1887, 10 p.c.; Lady Day 1888, 10 p.c.; Lady Day 1892, 10 p.c.; Michaelmas 1892, 10 p.c.	Since 1877 rents reduced £155 13s.; rents increased £13 10s.; total reduction. £142 3s.	—
A. H. Jones, for Rev. D. S. Jones and Mrs. Jones	Carmarthenshire (About 1000 acres)	In 1887 and 1888 an abatement of 10 p.c.	Two farms reduced 10 p.c. permanently	—
Mrs. Jones-Jones, Tibwrwen, Carmarthen	Elm Lodge (1805 acres in Carmarthen and Glamorgan)	For the years 1886 and 1887, 10 p.c.; the half-year ending Lady Day 1888, 10 p.c.; Lady Day 1892, 5 p.c.; Michaelmas 1892, 10 p.c.	No permanent reductions in rent since 1877	My estate has been valued twice; each time increasing my receipts

CARMARTHENSHIRE—(continued).

Name and Address of Landowner	Estate	Abatements	Reductions	Observations as to the History of Rents
Thomas Jones . . Llandovery	Carmarthenshire (965 acres)	I have this year allowed 10 p.c.	—	—
Capt. Jones-Parry . Tyllwyd, New-castle-Emlyn	Tyllwyd. (500 acres in Carmarthen)	Constantly. I have returned from 5 to 10 p.c.	—	The estate was re-valued in 1874. In one case there was a decrease; in the others some were unaltered; the rent increased, varying from 5 p.c. to 2 p.c. The increase was almost nominal. The property had not been valued since 1818, or perhaps before that even. Very large sums had been laid out in build-ings and improvements.
H. J. H. Lawrence Wannzron, Pem-brokeshire	Carmarthenshire (188 acres)	In 1892 I made an abatement of about 7½ p.c.	—	Within these last few years my farms have been re-valued, with the result of increasing the rent, but not up to the re-valuation
Mrs. Lawrence . Middleton Hall	Middleton Hall (2256 acres)	1886, 12½ p.c. on farm rents, 10 p.c. on park land for half-year ending December 24, 1885; 1886, 7½ p.c. on farms; 1887, 5 p.c. on park lands for half years ending June 24, 1886, December 24, 1886, June 24, 1887; 1888, Decem-	Have reduced the rents of three farms by £40, £18, and £12 respectively, and the rents of several divi-sions of the park by £66 10s., altogether making a total reduction of £136 10s. on the rent-roll. The land-	The estate was re-valued by three different valuers about 1878 or 1879 on account of a Chancery suit. As a whole have not had the rents of the lowest valuation. Some rents were raised by the late owner

Col. W. P. Llewellyn-Lewis, Llysnewydd, Llandyssil	Llysnewydd and Grange (4200 acres in Carmarthen and Cardigan)	her 24, 1887, June 24, 1888; 1889, 2¾ p.c. on farms, 2½ p.c. on park lands for half-year ending December 24, 1888; 1892, granted an abatement of £40 to one tenant who was in arrear, and let him the farm afterwards afresh at a rent reduced by £40; 1893, 10 p.c. on farms, 5 p.c. on park lands for half-year ending December 24, 1892	lord pays all outgoings on park lands, and does the fencing, and it is let as accommodation land	The estate was re-valued in 1871 by a most competent estate agent; the rents were raised *slightly* in some instances, but the rents generally are the same now as they were in 1871
Major C. B. Lewis, Aberystwyth	Cwmcloydach (785 acres)	My father, who died in 1890, granted abatements from 5 to 10 p.c. on several occasions. Last year I granted 5 p.c. and at the last audit for Michaelmas I granted 10 p.c.	In two or three cases	—
C. W. Mansel Lewis, Stradey Castle	Stradey Castle (4135 acres)	I returned 5 p.c. in the years 1885, 1886, and 1887, and in some cases 10 p.c. in the year 1892	Since the year 1877 I have permanently reduced my rents from 15 to 30 p.c., viz., farms reduced from £68 to £48 per annum; £62 to £45 per annum; £42 to £32 per annum; £70 to £50 per annum	—
		Abatements have been made this year, and since 1884 in three other years	—	—

APPENDIX.

CARMARTHENSHIRE—*(continued)*.

Name and Address of Landowner	Estate	Abatements	Reductions	Observations as to the History of Rents
David Jones Lewis . Llwynelyn, Llandovery	Gilfach and Llwynelyn	Abatements of rent granted at the audits of January 19, 1886; July 22, 1886; January 26, 1887; January 1888; July 22, 1892; January 18, 1893; on each occasion at the rate of 10 p.c.	Rents have been reduced in three cases, viz., from £33 to £30, from £75 to £60, and from £28 to £24	About 25 years ago the estate was re-valued. In most cases the rent was raised. In one case nothing was added to the rent except that the tithe rent-charge, which had been formerly paid by the landlord, was then laid upon the tenant. The general result of the valuation was an increase in the rents. Previous to this, as far as can be gathered, no increase of rents has taken place for at least two generations
John Lewis . Nantgwynne	Nantgwynne (400 acres)	For the last half-year only I have allowed them 10 p.c., and that is the general amount given by the other landowners, except a few cases where farms are rented high more is allowed. I have not been asked for abatements until this half-year's rent, which is entirely due to bad seasons and the loss of cattle and sheep	—	—

| Mrs. Lewis | Clynfew. (4870 acres in Pembroke, Cardigan, and Carmarthen) | 10 p.c. was given on the rents payable Michaelmas 1885 and Michaelmas 1892. Reductions have frequently been made at other times during the interval in *individual cases* | The estate has not been revalued for *purposes of rental*, but in the year 1888 a competent local valuer went over the whole property for the purpose of inspecting the state of repair and cultivation or re-arranging boundaries and re-adjusting values when necessary. The estate was at that time *very unequally let*, and the valuer advised a reduction in some cases and an increase in others. His recommendations were followed, but the rents were not raised to the figures mentioned by him in any one case, and in many cases no change was made at all. The net result of the valuation was a slight increase of the estate rental |
| Bishop of Llandaff, Llandaff | Henllan and Grove. (In Pembroke and Carmarthen, 3500 acres) | In 1886, 1887, 1888, and 1892 I returned 10 p.c. I succeeded to the properties in the year 1886 | Since 1886 I have made reductions in eight instances on the Henllan estate, amounting to the annual sum of £115. On the Grove estate reductions have been made in six instances, amounting to the annual sum of £120 | The estates have not been revalued for the last 50 years so far as I am aware. I have not raised the rent in any single instance since I became possessed of the estates |

CARMARTHENSHIRE—(continued).

Name and Address of Landowner	Estate	Abatements	Reductions	Observations as to the History of Rents
Geo. W. B. D. Lloyd Brunant, near Pumpsaint	Brunant	The late Mr. Lloyd granted allowances on each half-year's rents to the amount of 5 p.c. for some years previous to his death in 1887, but I cannot say for how many years. Since then reductions have been granted at the same rate at various times, and at the last rent audit a reduction of 10 p.c. was given	—	—
T. Lloyd-Barrow (for his wife, the owner of two-thirds of the Lloyd estate)	Lloyd. In Brecknock and Carmarthen, 4457 acres)	20 p.c. in November 1892; and 10 p.c. for the audit now due promised	—	—
Thos. Edward Lloyd. Coedmore, Cardigan	Coedmore and Trewern. (4500 acres in Cardigan, Carmarthen,and Pembroke)	For the Coedmore estate, 5 p.c. was allowed at Lady Day 1886, Michaelmas 1886, Lady Day and Michaelmas 1887, Lady Day and Michaelmas 1888, and Lady Day 1889 : and for Michaelmas 1892, 10 p.c. (except where there were leases). For the Trewern estate 10 p.c. was allowed at Michaelmas 1885, Lady Day 1886, Michaelmas 1886, Lady Day and Michaelmas 1887, Lady Day	I have not made any very material reductions of rent	

	Estate (acres)			
Capt. Tudor Lloyd-Harris Brynamlwg; Llandilo	Maesllydan and Trawsmawr. (5x11 acres in Carmarthen and Brecon)	Michaelmas 1885, Lady Day 1886, Michaelmas 1886, Lady Day 1887, Michaelmas 1887, Lady Day 1888, Lady Day 1892, Michaelmas 1892,10 p.c. allowed and Michaelmas 1888, 5 p.c. was allowed at Lady Day 1889, and 10 p.c. at Michaelmas 1892	In some cases rents are permanently reduced	The estate was re-valued in 1877; the result was a small increase in some places, not amounting to 3 p.c. on the rental
Mrs. E. F. Lloyd-Philipps Aberglasney, Golden Grove	Aberglasney (868 acres)	In 1892, 5 p.c.	Since 1877 I have reduced the rent of almost every farm	The estate was re-valued and rental increased some years since, but again reduced
Misses E. & E. J. Mansel	Maesteilo (1000 or 1100 acres)	When agricultural losses touched one's sympathy we have always been willing to listen to the tenant's appeal and make allowances, but in 1892 gave back 10 p.c. generally	One farm has been reduced £25, from £140 per annum	The estate has been re-valued, and in two farms only was there a slightly increased rental
E. W. Milner-Jones	Velindre (1800 acres)	10 p.c. last half-year	—	—
Howard Spear Morgan Tegfynydd	Tegfynydd, (1923 acres in Carmarthen and Pembroke)	Since times have been depressed returns of 10 p.c. have been made	No permanent reduction has been made except in some small holdings. The lands are all let at low rates	

CARMARTHENSHIRE—(continued).

Name and Address of Landowner	Estate	Abatements	Reductions	Observations as to the History of Rents
Herbert Peel . Taliaris, Llandilo	Taliaris (3000 acres)	10 p.c., half-year's rent due, Michaelmas 1885 : 5 p.c., Michaelmas 1886 : 5 p.c., Lady Day 1887 : 5 p.c., Michaelmas 1887 ; 10 p.c., Michaelmas 1892	Since I have come into this estate, which was in 1863, I have reduced the rents slightly in four cases, and have raised them slightly in three cases, thus reducing my rent-roll by £23	The rents were increased 10 p.c. in 1855. Since 1855 a few of the rents have been slightly raised in the changing of tenancy
(Late) John Peel Danyrallt, Llangadock	Danyrallt (3420 acres)	For the half-year ending Michaelmas 1885, an abatement of 20 p.c. For the two years ending Michaelmas 1887, of 10 p.c. For the half-year ending Lady Day 1888, of 10 p.c. For the half-year ending Michaelmas 1891, of 5 p.c. For one year ending Michaelmas 1892, of 15 p.c.	—	I purchased the bulk of these estates in the year 1881, and there has been no subsequent valuation for rental purposes. It is within my knowledge that there were several valuations of them made prior to my becoming the owner, but I have reason to know that these were made more for mortgage and sale purposes than for rental. In many cases the rents of farms were, on my becoming the owner, considerably lowered from the amounts alleged to have been previously paid
Wm. Lewis-Phillipps Clyngwynne	Clyngwynne (710 acres)	In 1887 and 1892 I gave a reduction of 5 p.c.	—	The property as a whole has not been re-valued within the last 50 years as far as I

Edward Sclaw Prothero, Dol-wilyu; Hebron	Dol-wilyn (About 1600 acres)	Abatements have been made in bad years—1882, 1885, 1886, 1887, and 1888—to about 5 or 6 p.c. In 1892 the tithe rent-charge was remitte l on a part of the estate for the year, and on the remainder for the half-year	In 1882 I reduced the rent of the largest farm 10 p.c., having granted lease of 21 years not long before. No addition was made to rent when lease fell in	The history of this small pro-perty is shortly this: in my grandfather's time farms were held on leases of three lives; these fell in in my mother's time, who suc-ceeded in 1841, and the farms were then re-valued. I succeeded in 1872. The only lease of lives fell in soon after, and that farm was then re-valued. I have since reduced it by 10 p.c.
A. P. Saunders-Davies Pentre, Boneath	Pentre. [6700 acres in Pembroke, Car-digan, and Car-marthen]			The Pentre old estate was valued about 30 years ago. Some of the farms were in-creased in rental and some reduced. The Pentre Uel-winkg estate was bought in 1884, and the rents have re-mained the same with the addition of the tithe
David E. Stephens Traws-mawr, Carnarthen	Part of Tra Us-mawr	Abatements of 10 p.c. were allowed on rentals of farms at several audits about 1885 and 1886. In some cases large re-ductions were made		know. The rents of these farms have been raised. Warnfawr, in consequence of extensive drainage, Pen-enwe, new purchase, after-wards drained. Waunfach, re-valued by tenant and rented at his own valuation

CARMARTHENSHIRE—(*continued*).

Name and Address of Landowner	Estate	Abatements	Reductions	Observations as to the History of Rents
Sir E. A. A. K. Cowell-Stepney, Llanelly	Stepney. (12,000 acres, chiefly in Carmarthen)	For three years, 1886-7-8, remitted 10 p.c.	Since 1877 we have not reduced our rents permanently, but they have not been raised for 50 years	It has been re-valued, but whether for the purposes of rental I do not know. Rents have been undisturbed on an average for about 50 years
John Crow Richardson, Glanbrydan Park, Manordilo.	Glanbrydan (1200 acres)	1885, 1886, 1887, 10 p.c. on each year to Michaelmas; 1888, 10 p.c. on half-year to Michaelmas; 1889, 5 p.c. on half-year to Michaelmas; 1892, 10 p.c. on one year to Michaelmas	—	If at any time a tenant thinks his rent too high and tells me so, I give him the opportunity of having the farm valued by a competent assessor, on the understanding that the annual value he may consider fair shall be the future rent, and in cases where this has been done the result has been in my favour
Mrs. Saunders, Court Henry, Golden Grove	Court Henry	No abatement required	—	The property was bought about 25 years ago. The tenants remained on at the same rents, and, from inquiries made, the rents were the same quite 20 years previously
David Thomas, Mile End, Llandovery	Carmarthenshire (320 acres)	Last Michaelmas rent I gave all my tenants an abatement of 10 p.c.; and at last Lady Day rent audit an abatement of 15 p.c. was given	In 1881 I made a permanent reduction of 20 p.c. to my tenant at Berthllwyd, and he had 10 p.c. last Michaelmas out of that reduced rent	—

David W. J. Thomas, Ely Cottage, Brecon	Hentlys. (1038 acres)	10 p.c. allowed at present, and in the depression in the years 1886, 1887, and 1888, the same was allowed	In 1863 the estate was re-valued by my father, when the rents were raised. Four valuers were employed at great expense. Each valued *separately*, and the *average* of the four valuations was adopted as the basis of the increase
John Thomas, Moreb, Llandilo	Tycanol. (128 acres)	—	—
John Lewes Thomas, Carglas, Llandilo	Carglas (1800 acres)	Returned 10 p.c. on last half-year's rent due Michaelmas day last	Have let the land at a reduction, from £140 per annum to £120, and again to £105 10s, for three years from September 29, 1891
Rhys Goring Thomas, Plas Llannon, Llanelly	Gellyweruen (1000 acres)	I have occasionally made a reduction of 10 p.c., but in no case permanent	Gellyweruen farm was reduced by £30 in the year 1880. It was formerly £210, now £180

CARDIGANSHIRE.

Thomas Harman Brenchley Glanoirw, Cardigan	Blaenporth (126 acres)	From July 1886 to January 1888, I returned 7½ p.c.; in 1889, 5 p.c.; January 1893, 5 p.c.	In 1880 I reduced the rent of principal farm £30 per annum, from £270 to £240

K

CARDIGANSHIRE—(continued).

Name and Address of Landowner	Estate	Abatements	Reductions	Observations as to the History of Rents
Mrs. Brigstocke. Blaenpant, Boncath	Blaenpant. (In Pembroke and Cardigan, 4900 acres)	In 1879, 10 p.c. from the Michaelmas rents; in 1881, 10 p.c. from the Michaelmas rents; and from 1885 to the present time 10 p.c. from every half-year's rent	I have permanently reduced the rents of three farms, one to the extent of £50 a year, another £15, and another £5	The estate has never been re-valued as a whole. There have been some increase of rent on change of tenancy
Earl Cawdor, Stackpole Court, Pembroke	In Carmarthen, Pembroke, and Cardigan, 70,000 acres	For three years, from Lady Day 1885 to Lady Day 1888, allowances of 15 p.c. were made to the farm tenants. For one year, from Lady Day 1891, the tithes have been allowed, being about 7½ p.c. For the present year, from Lady Day 1892, the tithes are again allowed, and an additional 10 p.c. out of the rents	No permanent reduction of any consequence up to the present time. Now a few trifling reductions are proposed.	All the estates were valued about 30 years back; and the rents were increased by re-lettings about £5000 a year
Major Parry Hughes and Mrs. Hughes, Allt-Lwyd, Abery-stwith	Allt-Lwyd and Malws. (In Cardigan and Pembroke, 3500 acres)	In some cases, 5 p.c.	All rents have been permanently reduced. Some instances : Farm £140 per annum for 50 years is reduced to £90, present rent Farm £180 per annum for 50 years is reduced to £130, present rent Farm £290 per annum for 40 years is reduced to £230,	The Allt-Lwyd estate was re-valued 5 years since : the old rents were reduced 16 p.c.

David Jones Tynyfyron Llanon, R.S.O.	Penlan. (165 acres)		present rent; and other farms have been reduced £10 and £5 per annum. These farms are upon the Allt-Lwyd estate, corn land, and were let by my father about 45 years since. No rents have been raised by me	Rent remained the same from 1841 to 1890
Mrs. Jones, Tiburwen, Carmarthen	Elm Lodge. (In Carmarthen and Cardigan, 1805 acres	For the years 1886 and 1887, 10 p.c.; the half-year ending Lady Day 1888, 10 p.c.; Lady Day 1892, 5 p.c.; Michaelmas 1892, 10 p.c.	Rent reduced in 1890 from £113 to £90; in 1893 from £90 to £80	My estate has been valued twice, each time increasing my receipts. In several instances rents have been raised
Captain Jones—Parry. Tyllwyd, Newcastle Emlyn	Tyllwyd (1208 acres)	Abatements are constantly granted. I have returned 5 to 10 p.c.		The estate was re-valued in 1874. In one case there was a decrease: in the others some were unaltered, the rent increased ranging from 5 to 2 p.c. The increase was almost nominal. The property had not been re-valued since 1818, or perhaps before that even. Very large sums had been laid out in buildings and improvements

CARDIGANSHIRE—(continued).

Name and Address of Landowner	Estate	Abatements	Reductions	Observations as to the History of Rents
Colonel John Lewis, Llanlear, Talsarn	Llanlear (1350 acres)	I have granted abatements of 10 p.c. in the years 1885, 1886, and 1887; in 1888, 7½ p.c.; in 1891, Michaelmas half-year, 10 p.c.; and in 1892, Michaelmas half-year, 10 p.c.	No reductions have been made	The estate was valued on the death of my father, in 1860. The valuation on the whole was an increase, but it had the effect of equalising the various holdings, which was much to be desired.
Colonel W. P. Llewelyn Lewes Llys-newydd, Llandyssil	Llysnewydd and Grange. (In Carmarthen and Cardigan, 4200 acres)	My father, who died in 1890, granted abatements from 5 to 10 p.c. on several occasions. Last year I granted 5 p.c. and at the last audit, for Michaelmas, I granted 10 p.c.	I have permanently reduced the rents in two or three cases; but the rents generally are the same now as they were when valued in 1871	The estate was valued in 1871, the rents being raised slightly in some instances.
Mrs. Lewis, Llysnewydd, Bonaeth	Clynfiew. (In Pembroke, Cardigan, and Carmarthen. 4870 acres)	Abatements have twice been granted; 10 p.c. was given on the rents payable Michaelmas 1885 and Michaelmas 1892. Reductions have frequently been made at other times during this interval in individual cases	A slight reduction has been made in the case of two farms, £5 a year on each	The estate has not been revalued for purposes of rental, but in the year 1888 a competent local valuer went over the whole property for the purpose of inspecting the state of repairs and cultivation, of re-arranging boundaries and readjusting values where necessary. The estate was at that time very unequally let, and the valuer advised a reduction in some cases and an increase in others. His recommenda-

Earl of Lisburne, Crosswood, Aberystwith	Crosswood (39,544 acres)	Considerable portions of the estates have been sold since 1888	The permanent reductions on my rent roll since 1877 amount to £573 14s.	tions were followed, but the rents were not raised to the figures mentioned by him in any one case, and in many cases no change was made at all. The net result of the valuation was a net result of the estate rental. My estates were re-valued as a whole for purposes of rental in my late father's time, in 1874, and the result was to increase the receipts. I entered into the possession of the estates in 1888, and made no re-valuation. I believe the rents of my property have not been raised in any particular instance except at the re-valuation
Thos. Edwd. Lloyd, Cocdmore, near Cardigan	Cocdmore and Trewern, (In Cardigan, Carmarthen, and Pembroke, 4500 acres)	For the Cocdmore estate, 5 p.c. was allowed in Lady Day 1886, Michaelmas 1886, Lady Day and Michaelmas 1887, Lady Day and Michaelmas 1888, and Lady Day 1889; and for Michaelmas 1892, 10	Since 1877 rents have not been reduced very materially	The Trewern estate was re-valued in 1864, for the purpose of a partition between my late mother and uncle, Mr. Longcroft, of Llanina, Cardiganshire, and such valuation has not been mate-

£ s. d.

10 p.c., half-year to Michaelmas 1885   544 19 1

10 p.c., one year to Michaelmas 1886   1119 15 6

10 p.c. one year to Michaelmas 1887   1140 16 5

12½ p.c. one year to Michaelmas 1888   1472 4 7

15 p.c., one year to Michaelmas 1889   1661 3 10

10 p.c., half-year to Michaelmas 1892   377 19 3

6316 18 8

CARDIGANSHIRE—(continued).

Name and Address of Landowner	Estate	Abatements	Reductions	Observations as to the History of Rents
Thos. Edwd. Lloyd Coedmore, near Cardigan—cont.		p.c. (except where there were leases). For the Trewern estate, 10 p.c. allowed at Michaelmas 1885 and Lady Day 1886; the same Michaelmas 1886, the same at Lady Day and Michaelmas 1887, the same at Lady Day and Michaelmas 1888, 5 p.c. was allowed at Lady Day 1889; and 10 p.c. at Michaelmas 1892		rially altered since that period, except in cases where old leases have fallen in
Capt. Herbert Vaughan Brynog, Talsarn	Brynog. (2800 acres)	10 p.c. some half-dozen audits	Since the passing of the Tithe Act in 1891 I pay the tithe, and in rearranging the rents, my income is reduced by some £50	Every farm of mine has a field valuation made some 30 years ago, but in no instance has any farm been let at a rental as high as the valuation
Mrs. Vaughan Llangoedmore Cardigan	Llangoedmore (550 acres)	I returned 5 p.c. to my tenants when they paid their rents in 1887, and paid a half-year's tithe rent-charge for each tenant in 1892	I have not permanently reduced my rents since 1877. One small holding only was reduced from £14 to £10	—
T. J. Waddingham Hafod, near Aberystwith	Hafod. (In Cardigan and Montgomery, 15,000 acres)	For the two last half-years 10 or 15 p.c. has been allowed to all who paid punctually	After 1877 the rents of those who had no leases were permanently reduced by 10 p.c. To the largest tenant (3000 to 4000 acres) besides	The estate has not been valued during the time for which I have known it, viz., 22 years. The rent of one newly-purchased farm was raised, but

Owner	Estate (acreage)	Abatement	Reductions	Remarks
Mrs. Lloyd Phillpps. Penty Park, Haverfordwest	664 acres	For the last four or five years 10 p.c.	the 10 p.c. reduction of rent, £100 was allowed in 1885 for that year, and last year his rent was reduced by £30. The permanent reduction has been about 38 p.c. I should add that from 17 to 18 p.c. of the rents are paid by hauling for the landlord at so much a load	buildings have since been erected thereon
Arthur Picton Saunders-Davies, Pentre, Boncath	Pentre, (In Pembroke, Cardigan, and Carmarthen. 6700 acres)	No abatements	No reductions — In one case the rent of a farm was reduced from £90 to £80	The Pentre old estate was revalued about 30 years ago. Some of the farms were increased in rental and some reduced. The Pentre Cilwendeg estate was bought in 1884, and the rents have remained the same, with the addition of the tithe
Captain Stewart Alltrodyn	Alltrodyn (1123 acres)	In 1888 an abatement of 5 p.c., and in 1893 of 10 p.c. on all farms	In 1887 reduced the rent of Blaencinon £10, from £35 to £75; in 1888 reduced the rent of Pwllbryn £4, from £34 to £30, tenant to expend £4 yearly in lime	—

Printed by BALLANTYNE, HANSON & Co.
London & Edinburgh